THE WHITE HEART

THE WHITE HEART
A PROCESS OF CREATIVE INCUBATION

SHIRLEY LYONS

Order this book online at www.trafford.com
or email orders@trafford.com

Most Trafford titles are also available at major online book retailers.

Acknowledgements:
Sri Aurobindo Ashram Trust, Pondicherry, for permission to use quotes of the Mother and photos of the Mother and Sri Aurobindo.
Photo of Matrimandir: S. Rajan.
Photopgraph of Author F. Zubicary Bask Country
Book Cover: Shirley Lyons & Tixon Mohan

Printed in the United States of America.

ISBN: 978-1-4269-4039-2 (sc)
ISBN: 978-1-4269-4040-8 (hc)
ISBN: 978-1-4269-7721-3 (e)

Library of Congress Control Number: 2010911498

Trafford rev. 05/17/2012

 www.trafford.com

North America & international
toll-free: 1 888 232 4444 (USA & Canada)
phone: 250 383 6864 ♦ fax: 812 355 4082

To: The Mother
And to
My Children - who stood firm
throughout the process-

Acknowledgements:

Sri Aurobindo Ashram Trust, Pondicherry,
for permission to use quotations of the Mother and photographs
of the Mother and Sri Aurobindo
Photograph of Matrimandir: S. Rajan, Auroville
Photograph of Author: F. Zubicaray, Bask Country
Book Cover design: Shirley Lyons & Tixon Mohan, Auroville

Preface

This book is not about the lives of Sri Aurobindo and the Mother. It is merely an introduction to who They are and how They changed my life. Sri Aurobindo came to me in the form of an apparition and I spent four years trying to find out who He was. I met the Mother and at the same time found Him. Through the process of finding Them, I found myself. My story is about the process (lessons), which took forty years of constant vigilant trials and errors in observing who I am.

I want to thank profoundly all of my friends and acquaintances who helped me during the seven years of developing this manuscript. Without each of them I would have been lost in a maze of uncertain words. They read, corrected, and encouraged me to complete this work. Their kindness and patience will forever be a part of my life.

The Mother

"If one sincerely wants to help others and the world, the best thing one can do is to be oneself what one wants others to be, not only by example, but because one becomes a center of radiating power which, by the very fact that it exists, compels the rest of the world to transform itself."

The Mother: Questions and Answers 1957-58, pp. 416-17

"If you go deep enough where all outer things are as silent as can be you will find within that flame of which I often speak, and in that flame you will seek your destiny."

The Mother: Questions and Answers 1954, pp. 271-72

"The effort which you will be able to make individually, instead of being only an individual progress, will spread; it will have very important collective results.

The Mother: Questions and Answers 1957-58, pp.172-73

Introduction

The purpose of this book is to give birth to an awareness of the potential available for each human being to advance beyond the controlling power of the physical, emotional, and mental minds. This transformation is a slow, creative journey which can be greatly accelerated when one understands the need to develop into a higher consciousness. Personal experience has led me to believe transformation is a necessary process we must undergo to become even greater beings than ever we believed possible. I was a "plain Jane" from the Midwest of the USA. I have changed enormously since then. If this happened to me, it can happen to anyone who dares to step out of their human binding.

It has been suggested to me that many of the experiences that I relate are holy and should not be told because they are secret and will lose their power in the telling. My response is this: the time has come when universal human potential needs to be more fully understood, because what is possible for one person is possible for all.

What is obvious, at least I hope it is obvious, is the fact that modern society is going through a tremendous change. In the West especially, we are struggling with an ever increasing pace of life. At the same time, other parts of the world are still on hold.

Life for them hasn't changed at all. Starvation and war are a constant threat. I have lived in seven countries on four continents, and in too many places evidence of man's inhumanity to man was devastating.

In 1967 I was forced to wake up. I was shaken and taken into a new reality. This book is my story, a crack in my cosmic egg. It has taken more than thirty years of an ongoing process, a creative incubation, to peel off the layers of mud and darkness.

But somehow, somewhere there was always a spark of light to illuminate the way. My wish is that this book will be of a quality that adequately expresses my sincere gratitude, humility, and acknowledgement of the inspiring work of Sri Aurobindo and the Mother. I graciously thank Them, and others, like Jim Goure, and Alex for the sparks that ignited my soul.

PART ONE – My Story

(A true story. Some names and places have been changed.)

Lesson One – An Apparition

I was born in Holland, Michigan, seventy-nine years ago in 1930, into a Dutch Christian Reformed family. From the ages of eight through eleven, my brother and I would spend every weekend at the home of my very religious grandparents. On Sundays our weekly routine began by my grandfather driving us to a large, red brick, church at nine o'clock in the morning. We entered and filed down the aisle to the third row from the front. We spent two hours sitting on a hard church pew, chewing two peppermints (half-way into the sermon) and listening to an overactive preacher deliver the hell, fire and damnation sermon. At eleven o'clock my brother and I would race each other down the steps to the basement for another hour of Sunday school. Later, at home, when the noon meal was finished and we were still seated at the table, my grandfather would continue his zealous religious training. He read a chapter from the Bible and before we were excused, we had to answer questions about what he had read. If we (and that included my grandmother), responded inaccurately, he would re-read the chapter and re-ask the questions. Needless to say, we three became good listeners.

The next regular Sunday event was to dry the dishes after lunch, which my grandmother had washed, and to then get ready to walk or ride the ten, long, city blocks back to church. We attended an hour of CE (a children's Christian Endeavor Program). My grandfather drove us to CE both during the cold winter months and whenever I had to carry my heavy saxophone to play a song in church. My brother kept telling me to volunteer to play my sax so that we would get a ride. At seven thirty on Sunday evenings, we were very happy to go to bed early, rather than attend yet another later church service.

During those formative years, I would frequently complain to my mother about how long and boring the preacher's sermons were. Her response was always the same. "You are very lucky. When I was a child, those two hours were in Dutch!"

My early religious experience continually reminded me that I, a mere child, was a sinner. That statement perplexed and angered me. I kept asking myself what sin I had committed. Could it be the cookies I would sometimes sneak from the cookie jar? Was it that each time I had to walk to Christian Endeavor I would stop at the gas station and spend half of my collection money on a candy bar? None of it made much sense to me, so I wasn't a strong believer in a God who appeared not to like me.

One bright Sunday morning, from out of nowhere, this tedious ritual was interrupted by something extremely exciting. I was seated between my grandparents in the pew. The preacher was fully launched into his usual sermon. Suddenly, to my utter amazement, I heard a very clear and precise spoken voice that came from inside or above the right side of my head speak to me. That voice said "Everyone is going to become A Jesus. Not Jesus, but A Jesus!" I shuddered with inner shock and alerted fear. Had my grandmother, whose ear was inches from mine, heard what I had just heard? If so, I was in real trouble. How dare I believe that we can be compared to Jesus! I glanced at my grandfather. His eyes were not staring back into my eyes. I was safe. I could keep my secret.

It was over twenty-five years later in 1967, on the seventh day of the seventh month, when I had just turned thirty-seven years old, that a voice came to me again. My husband was away on a business trip, and I was in a new apartment in Barcelona, Spain, with my daughter and son. I had also had another daughter, my first child who had died in her sleep. This death weight heavily on me even years later. What happened next had a direct bearing on that regrettable day. I was sleeping in a bedroom that had double doors. They opened onto the living room, through which I could see the double glass doors which opened from the living room onto the terrace. I could not see what was happening in the next room. I was awakened at dawn on that peaceful morning by what sounded like the flapping of wings. Listening more intently, it sounded as if something was flying around and around near the ceiling in the living room. Looking at the terrace doors and wondering if a bird was in the house because someone had mistakenly left the doors open the night before, it was a complete surprise to find them still closed. From my bed, elbow bent with my head raised on my hand, so I could tip my right ear to hear more clearly, the flapping sounds became more and more rapid. Soon there was the sound of what I can only describe as a whirlwind of twirling energy. It sounded as if a hurricane was coming. I thought, "It's a Hurricane!" Out on the terrace not one plant leaf moved. Suddenly I blurted: "Oh no, it's a flying saucer!" The force of a whizzing disk with a swooshing sound was lowering itself down on the tipped right side of my head and face. I grabbed my right ear. It burned with a tremendous heat. As this was occurring, a clear voice said, "Don't be afraid. The agony of your life is over. Nothing is going to happen to these children."

THE MYSTERY MAN

I looked up and there in the corner of the room blinking off and on for some time as if it were on a large, poster size, black and white television screen, was an image of a man that looked like a portrait. He had very intense, dark eyes, long dark hair and, what seemed strange for a man so young, a very wire-like white beard. Sitting up in bed, slightly slapping my face to make sure I was wide awake, the words "What is going on? Who is this man? came into my head.

Answering myself, sprang the words, "I don't know who this foreigner was, but I think He was a philosopher who lived in the eighteen hundreds. He looked Italian."

While watching in wonderment, I experienced three human sensations: intense heat, hearing a voice, and seeing a face. I knew it was real, that I hadn't conjured it up, it all happened so suddenly. What did it mean? I wasn't crazy, just dumbfounded. This was an apparition! Are they really real? Who would believe me? And what, if anything, did it mean?

This experience didn't feel religious because, if so, why didn't Jesus come to me? Christianity was the only religion I knew. Since we were in Spain, I wondered if maybe some Spanish ghost was flying around in the neighborhood. My biggest unanswered question was, "Why me?" I wasn't afraid, just curious. How could I possibly describe or convey the state of bewilderment I found myself in that evening? Now the house was quiet and there was time to think. Is seeing a ghost a believable reality? Who was this mysterious man? Was His voice the same voice that had come to me years ago while sitting in church as an eleven year old child? I was consumed with the strangeness of the whole affair.

Still, strange occurrences of this kind were not new to me. Throughout my life I had often heard my family discuss weird, unusual happenings, and an experience like hearing a voice might be just another one of those crazy incidents. That evening, I sat in a lounge chair on a dimly-lit terrace, recollecting two major, not so common events.

Many years before, my mother told me about her youngest brother, Dennis. Her parents and her seven sisters and brothers moved from Kalamazoo, Michigan, to another Dutch town, Holland, Michigan. After settling in a new house, Dennis told my grandmother he would never go to school in this new town. My grandmother replied, "Don't be that way, of course you will go to school here. Don't worry, you will meet new friends at your new school and you will be happy here." He was nine years old.

Dennis died of pneumonia before school started in the fall. While he was in the hospital and near death, he said to those around his bedside, "Don't cry, there are angels lined up to take me. Can't you see them? Can't you hear their beautiful music? Please don't cry."

How did Dennis know it was his time to die? Because he did know!

I had been told that story, but was a witness to the latter part of the next one. The nightmarish saga had started when my mother made an unfortunate, and unguarded remark, a remark which would trouble her for the next twenty years of her life. At that time I was twenty-four months old and very ill because of an ulcer in my left eye. I couldn't hold food in my stomach and, because of the Depression, was without proper nourishment. She kept me alive on rice water. She held me when she did the dishes, even when she went to the toilet. If she put me down, I would cry and she thought crying drained my energy, so she constantly held me in her arms.

The doctor came to the house to examine me, and he said to my mother, "Prepare yourself, this child may not live through the night." She shouted, "Get out! If you can't say something good: say nothing. This child is going to live. It is that baby in the crib who will never live to be twenty-one!" My brother died six months before his twenty-first birthday. My mother lived twenty agonizing years waiting for him to turn twenty-one.

The strangeness of my brother's death has to do with this theme of unusual happenings. He had just come home from college and because my mother wanted him to hang around the house, rather than go out drinking, she had bought him a rowboat. Since we lived on a lake, and the fish would bite early in the morning, it meant going to bed early to get up early to catch fish. My brother was sitting at home waiting to go to bed at around ten o'clock in the evening, but he got thirsty, so he went next door to get a soda at my uncle's boat and bait shop. While there, a car pulled up to buy gas and my brother recognized his best friend's brother, who he knew was on furlough from the Marine Corps. My brother didn't know any of the other people in the car, but because of the Marine he accepted their invitation to go to a local hangout for a late night snack. While there, he ran into another uncle and they had a short chat. On the way home, the young man driving the car decided to play "chicken." He turned off the car lights and where the road curved he went straight and slammed the car into a huge tree. The three young men in the back seat were killed instantly. My brother was one of them. My uncle, my mother's other brother who lived near us, was driving behind them. If only my brother had gone home with him.

At the moment of my brother, Duane's, death, my mother was also driving a car with a friend in the seat beside her. She suddenly pulled the car over to the side of the road, turned off the lights, slumped over, and went into another state of awareness.

"I was in a meadow of beautiful, beautiful flowers," she said when she came to. Then she started up the car and drove on.

When they arrived at the restaurant on the lake, she went into the Ladies room. As she passed through the doorway, she had to tightly grab on to the door frame because she thought she was going to faint. She felt a very forceful vibration come up from her feet, go through her body and out of her head.

It wasn't long after that my uncle called with the bad news, telling her that Duane was in the hospital. On the way to the hospital my mother kept repeating, "It's too late, it's too late. I know that it is too late. He's dead. I know that he's dead!"

She tried to open the car door in order to jump out to take her own life, but her friend grabbed her.

With my mother barely able to function, the responsibility of the funeral was given to me. One evening I sat down in the

9

large living room easy chair to select a song to be sung. I placed the closed hymnal on my lap. While adjusting my legs to get more comfortable, and with no effort on my part, the book opened. It was like phantom hands had selected a page that read, "Just as I Am Without One Plea." Wow! It struck me like a perfect thought. This is the absolute perfect song for Duane. To this day, I believe that those phantom hands that opened that hymnal were my brother's and that he chose that song because of the words to be sung.

After my brother's death and upon returning to my apartment in Mexico City, my friends found me an emotional basket case. I had returned to finish my degree at art school, but my mind was still at home. Figuring out what human phenomenon allowed my mother to predict her child's future death never escaped me. I felt such agony for her to have had to live for twenty years with the constant reminder that her child might not have a full life. She lived with the hope that what she had uncontrollably uttered, "He will never live to be twenty-one," would never occur. My sorrow for her and myself was overwhelming.

At twenty-two, I had to get back into the swing of returning to classes. After a short period of time, and with much concern for my mental health, a fellow classmate from Chicago felt that I should go to see her therapist. She explained that he charged only what people could afford, and for students that wasn't much. She wanted no excuse that I couldn't pay his fee. She took me to our first meeting and then she left.

A full hour later, and with a session of nothing but tears, the therapist said, "That is the easiest money I have ever made. I want you to rent a boat in Chapultepec Park and sit there until you have filled the pond with your tears. When you have finished, come back and see me again."

I lived just across the street from Chapultepec Park, near the statue Diana, so it was very easy for me to take his advice.

When I returned to see him, after six sessions he said, "You don't need me. Just forget your childhood of the Dutch Reformed Religion and enjoy life."

That night I had a dream. It was one of those dreams you never forget. Each time you recall it, you re-live it in all its original vividness. In the dream I was standing under a street light at a crossroad which went in four directions. Each street I looked down, led to darkness. It was black to the north, south, east, and west of me. I didn't know in which direction to go. In a field between two of the streets was a small cottage with all of the lights on. The front door was wide open. I knew going through that door would bring me love and security. Standing there, stuck in my tracks, in all directions except the cottage I faced the unknown.

After what seemed a long time, I finally stepped out of the shadow of myself, under the street light, and into the darkness. I woke up, rolled over to the edge of the bed, gasped, and groaned with dry heaves. I thought I was dying.

Death seemed to hang over my head from as far back as I can remember, forever opening questions without answers. My father died in World War II when I was thirteen. My brother, the only other child in the family, died when I was twenty-two. My first child died when I was thirty-one. Now, at thirty-seven, a strange ghost-man with a mystical voice was visiting me. I looked to make a connection. My mind kept asking, "What on earth is life and death about, and what am I supposed to realize in my experience with both?"

Intuitively, I knew my life had changed. Here I was near the middle of my life, sitting on a lighted terrace in front of an apartment in Barcelona, facing the unknown and realizing once again my world was being transformed forever.

Lesson Two – Death Is Energy

Once the overseas assignment for my husband's work terminated, we moved back to the United States and immediately rented a sublet in Greenwich Village, located on the lower west side of Manhattan. His work would now have him travel overseas for two or three weeks at a time. He knew of my experience with the apparition in Barcelona and since he had been interested in Theosophy in college, he was open to the possibility of my new found wonderment. I was free to investigate any ideas I felt compelled to know.

While he was away, I devoured books on any material of which I knew nothing. It was the sixties and there were lots of weird new-age ideas floating around. I read about religions, philosophy, reincarnation (which immediately made sense), astral projection, ESP, psychometry, and yoga. You name it, I read it. However, the one topic that escaped my attention was the subject of the White Light.

One day while my children were playing in the next room, I lay face down on the bed to have a short rest. It wasn't safe to fall asleep because the children were young enough to get into trouble. As soon as my eyes closed, my body seemed to slowly drift across water. With a feeling of weightlessness, my body moved above the waves while undulating to a definite rhythm. For a moment, I wondered if I was going to get seasick.

Then upward over an island I soared, continually rising up, up and away until fusing with an all-encompassing White Light. The feeling was without boundaries of time or space. Words cannot describe the sensation because there was no thought or the processing of thought, just a constant glow of natural joy and peace. "There is a Peace That Passes Understanding Down in My Heart," an old Sunday school song came to mind as I soared in that netherworld that defied understanding. Unexpectedly, I heard a voice, a real voice, my son's voice.

"Hey, Shirley!" (My child, Noah, always called me by my first name.) "Where's my truck?" His voice brought me back to reality, and I wondered how long I had been away.

When my husband returned home and I described my new experience to him, his response was, "Why you?" Which I had learned by then actually meant "Why not me?" and this added strain to our relationship. He had difficulty coming to terms with the fact that, as a student of Theosophy with a more academic mind, he, rather than I, should have had this happen to him.

Our marriage was undergoing a series of problems, the most demanding one being dealing with the death of a child. This experience in a marriage can either bring a couple closer together, or send them oceans apart. In our case, it sent us apart and it was probably mostly my fault. Death had seriously wounded me. I couldn't shake the puzzlement of the mystery surrounding the prediction of my brother's death or the stupidity of the way he died. When our child passed away in her sleep on Christmas Eve, for me, it was the straw that broke the camel's back. Death had a hold on me.

Day and night I carried death on my shoulders. I walked the streets of Madrid, Spain, in a state of depression, with thoughts of ending my own life. I would speak to myself as I crossed them, saying "Now! Throw yourself in front of this car. Do it, now!"

For days on end, I walked and cried, but I had a four-week-old baby at home and had to live for her. I tried not to give in to my hurt. Two months later, my grandmother, who had been like a mother to me, died. Calling out to God didn't help because I had given up on God. Call out, why? My loved ones were leaving me so quickly. My loved ones were gone, gone, gone. Nothing I could imagine would ease my pain.

That is, until something happened to change my mind and my way of thinking about loss.

Years ago, back in the United States, when teaching elementary school in California, a colleague and I grew close enough to pledge to see one another every ten years of our lives. A decade ago, she had come to visit me in England. And now it was time for me to fly from New York to Oceanside, California, to make a return on our promise. So I did.

Early one evening of my visit, we went to a restaurant along the water. When we arrived, the dining area was fully occupied. Consequently, we waited at the bar, having a drink until a table became available. I was paying attention to my friend who was jabbering in my ear, and the bartender who was washing and clinking small glasses near my face, but I was tempted to focus my attention on a huge picture window looking over the peaceful Pacific Ocean.

Out of nowhere, one of the clouds in the very blue sky spoke to me. Yes, spoke to me. Not a voice as I had heard before in my Barcelona room, but a decisive pronouncement of thought that said, "Death is energy and energy is non-ending."

With those words, my body immediately reacted. As if someone had turned off a light switch, the cells of my body that were then hyper-sensitized by otherworldliness simply shut down. But so what? I knew that I had experienced truth, and without fully realizing it, the vibration of my cells.

My burden of death was forever lifted. It was a remarkably freeing moment. I learned to forget death. I was free. I intuitively knew that our bodies are just the vehicles that transfer energy, like water does in becoming ice or a vapor.

Lesson Three – A Cornered Mind

My husband and I eventually decided on a trial separation. It was 1974 and for him, it meant living the good life in New York City, while also traveling the world in first class hotels. He would come to visit the children on holidays, birthdays, and whenever he was on a business trip in our area. For me, it was another kind of death.

As much as I enjoyed my two children, having lived away from America for over ten years to experience an alternate lifestyle, and being away from all of my friends had been a real adjustment. Abroad we had a good life with expense accounts, maids, and cultural and intellectual stimulation. Now, at forty-four, I was back in Michigan, my childhood stomping grounds, so that I could be with my mother, whom I thought needed me as much as I needed her.

Coming home took as much of an adjustment as leaving. I wasn't sure where I fit in anymore.

My mother had lost her husband, her son, and the money from a business she had recently sold. She turned to alcohol to help get her through her days, lived on a widow's pension, and dreamed that her next wildcat oil well would come in and make us all rich.

My children were in the first and third grades, and I was a substitute teacher. I felt I needed to occupy my mind, so once again I returned to the puzzle of the mysterious apparition.

There were yoga classes in Grand Rapids, and during the process of signing up for a class, because of the questions I asked, the instructor suggested I try mental Raja Yoga, rather than the more physical Hatha Yoga. She gave me the names of two women that she thought might be able to help me. I called the first lady that night and she invited me to come to see her at seven o'clock the next evening.

It did not take me long to understand something magical was taking place in my life on that visit the following evening.

Upon being seated in my instructor's living room, the whole area lit up. There were streams of light glowing from and around her body.

I introduced myself and said, "Please, give me a moment to adjust to your White Light," to which she replied, "Thank you."

That year Nellie and I became good friends. We had many fascinating discussions about the Spiritual Masters of the White Brotherhood. On that topic she didn't arouse much of my interest, but she turned me on to many other spiritual groups. She soon introduced me to Spiritual Frontiers Fellowship (SFF). Attending their meetings was always exciting because I learned so many new things.

The second woman I was referred to conducted weekly evening, group sessions. At one of her meetings, I met a visitor who was a guest of one of the large department stores in our town. He was a young hair stylist who would be giving appointments to the public for the next two weeks. He needed a ride back to his hotel, which was located a few blocks from my neighborhood, so we drove home together. He turned out to be a very interesting individual because he had traveled the world with the famous singer, Dinah Washington.

A local newspaper article about him revealed that he was a psychometrist. He would take a piece of jewelry you had worn daily for years and read the vibrations that emanated from it. He had some free evenings and so did I, so we often met at a local coffeehouse and had many long discussions.

During one of these discussions, he told me about an incident that had happened at his workplace. An elderly woman who was employed at the store came to him and asked if he believed in ghosts. (Ghosts! My ears quickly perked up) He arranged to meet her in the lunchroom cafeteria during their next coffee break and this is the story she told:

Every weekend she and her daughter would drive to their cottage on Lake Michigan. They would make a fire in the fireplace and stay overnight.

One Sunday, while they were driving away from the cottage, They noticed one of the lights was on. They were positive all of the lights had been turned off. They drove back and turned off the light.

As they were driving away this second time, her daughter said, "I had the strangest feeling that Tom was in the house this weekend."

Her Mother reacted, "So did I."

Tom was her son who had been an intelligence officer in the military service. He was killed in Vietnam.

The following weeks when they would make a fire in the fireplace, the smoke would drift upward and collect in the form of the top-half of a person. They recognized it as Tom. They began to talk to him and he would answer. He told them he was okay and not to worry about him.

Tom said he had died because his real work was on the other side. It was his responsibility to help young GIs who had been taught to kill, and then they themselves had been killed, to realize they no longer had a body. The GIs kept roaming and searching for their loved ones on earth. Tom calmly guided them to a state of peace. This lady and her daughter asked her son's ghost many questions and most of them he couldn't answer because he said the information would be beyond human understanding.

These kinds of stories fascinated me, and joining like-minded people during workshops and conventions became a way of bringing a renewed interest into what I perceived as a very dull life–my own. My spiritual curiosity needed to be fed, and attending SFF monthly meetings opened a chance to keep abreast of the views of speakers about new, old, and far-out ideas. Nothing was too far-out!

During one SFF meeting, I met Alex, an American guru (Raja Yoga teacher), from Illinois. He held retreats at his center and in Michigan. At a retreat, I sat next to him while he performed a ceremony called "The Ring of Fire." During the ceremony, the group sat in a circle while holding hands. The guru transferred to me, the person sitting next to him, a feeling of waves of energy. As it passed through my hands, I sent it on to the next person. When it came to the end of the circle and back to the guru, he recharged it and passed it on again. This circular motion continued for some time until each person in the group was supercharged with spiritual energy.

When the meeting ended, I quickly drove home, got two small onyx-stone birds that came from Mexico, returned and placed them in the guru's hands. As he took this insignificant gift, I had no idea as to why he should have something from me. I just felt the impulse to give him something I was attached to, something personal.

His reaction stunned me. He smiled and said, "Now you can be my student."

We sat alone in silence and he initiated me into his line of gurus. At that time, the initiation had almost no impact on me, but later that night the import of it surfaced. There was a sensation of a flame around my heart. It burst into colored vibrations that slowly subsided.

After jumping out of bed and taking out my paints, my version of the event was recorded on watercolor paper.

The following night, there was another magical event. An explosion of colors awoke me. A huge zinnia-like flower appeared above my brain. I saw petals spread in a circle across the entire top of my head.

On the third evening, the same flower blossomed, but this time the colors were magnificently otherworldly. I wondered if this was what happened to people who took drugs, because I certainly would have loved to experience this sensation over and over again. The intensity of the velvet-like colors was startlingly new to me.

A short time later, I heard that a guru who was a friend of Alex, the guru from Illinois, was giving a Yoga Retreat in upstate New York. My mother watched the children and fortunate me enrolled in the yoga classes and prepared myself for a wonderful week of peace and harmony.

At the retreat, we meditated at sunrise and did Hatha yoga exercises. In the evening we listened to a lecture by the guru. Five days of quiet, light food, exercise, and meditation put me in a very receptive state of being. I was anxiously anticipating an upcoming lecture entitled, "You Can Control Your Mind," that proved to be everything I had hoped it would be.

After the lecture, the guru's parting words were, "You can ask your mind to interpret your dreams."

My reaction was, "That is so cool! I am going to my room to dream." And dream I did.

My husband's family owned an old-style, kosher hotel near Cape May, New Jersey. In the dream, I was standing on the second floor porch of the hotel, throwing out all of the personal belongings of the family: baby shoes, high chairs, furniture, toys, etc. As fast as I got rid of things, my husband's two aunts, who were sitting in rocking chairs on the ground floor front porch, would bring them back inside.

The scene in the dream quickly changed. I was now in my New York apartment holding the door open while workmen carried out my precious antiques.

At that moment I remembered I could ask my mind to interpret the dream. I said, "OK mind, what is the meaning of this dream?"

My mind answered, "You are throwing away antique ideas and making way for the new."

I thought, "Wow, this is great! I can talk to my own mind!"

Suddenly, within the deep center of my inner being, an interplay of ideas took shape. It was something outside of my mind. It was a witnessing of something more than my mind.

"Hey, who said 'OK mind, what is the meaning of this dream?'"

Indeed, who or what (if it wasn't my mind), inside of me questioned my own mind? Was it another aspect of mind? Was it my soul or my consciousness? Who am I, if not my mind?

I later learned that this being, which is part of me, is called the witness.

The next night, I happily dreamed again. This time, in the dream my head was expanding. The upper top back of my head was slowly blowing up like a balloon. It kept getting bigger and bigger. My thoughts automatically told me, "You are pregnant in the head." I knew what giving birth was all about and in no way did I want to experience that as a cerebral experience. Nonetheless, I still felt like my head was going to explode.

While panicking and wanting to race down the hall to the room of the guru, to knock on his door and yell, "Help, help," I cautiously calmed down. I sat up the rest of that early morning and didn't meditate again for months. I was afraid of my own cosmic ability.

When you are a novice and play around with your mind, you can go to a lot of unexpected places. That is the reason I was never tempted to take drugs. In the first place, you frighten yourself because you are entering into unchartered territory within your head. Your mind doesn't want you exploring. It has complete control over all facets of your being and it doesn't want to lose its power to properly influence you, so it fights back. It knows all of your weaknesses and all of the idiosyncrasies of the weaknesses of your physical, emotional, and mental minds. When it doesn't use one mind, it will use another just to keep you controlled and confused.

I was very careful to give proper respect to my mind. Whenever I sat down to meditate, I would try to make a friend of my mind, prepare it and care for it, so it wouldn't feel the need to fight back. I would instruct my mind to allow me to have time for myself. I would say, "Mind, take a break. This is time for me to be by myself. Go sit in a corner and be quiet until this meditation has ended. Soon I will call you back and we will be together again."

If during meditation a thought would come to my mind, I would remind it to go back in the corner and be quiet until I was ready to call it back. If thoughts persisted, I would very forcefully command them to return to the corner. "Get back to your corner!"

At first, it was a constant war, but after a long period I began to attain a degree of silence. Confidence and trust edged into my meditations. My mind wasn't about to give in easily. It continued to fight back, to challenge for control of myself. It tormented me every hour that I was awake.

Sometimes my brain area ached. I would look in the mirror and feel where my brain left off and my face began. Relentlessly, it kept it up, searching out past fears and doubt.

"Look at you. You have lost everything. Your friends are happily married. Your husband is out having fun, living the good life. You have no sex life, no money, no future, nothing."

On and on it went, and I couldn't shut it off. I had never heard of scream therapy, but at night when everyone was sleeping, I would get in my car and drive around the town screaming at the top of my voice, "Shut up! Leave me alone! Give me some peace!" Then one day it did.

It was an evening after supper. I was lying on the carpet in the living room. There was a cozy fire in the fireplace and my daughter was happily playing while sitting on my back. I nonchalantly looked up and there in the corner of the room I saw two thick, long, white plastic-like tubes. Hooked together they formed a corner. Each tube had a separate opening. Out of the openings came gasping sounds. The sounds were like the utterance of choking or panting, a creature struggling to breathe. I slowly asked myself, "What does this mean?"

The answer came easy enough, much easier than my struggle to free myself from my thoughts. "You have cornered your mind."

My inner self, the witness, said to me, "Finally, you have taken control."

Lesson Four – Initiation

Educational philosophy had always fascinated me. I attended workshops on the methodology of Maria Montessori, the Waldorf School of Rudolph Steiner, and Summer Hill of Alex Neill. The ideas of Marla Collins, Mortimer Adler, and Jonathan Kozol evoked great admiration.

I had been a child who never fit into the public school system. Reading, spelling, and math remained difficult. I excelled in art, gym, and music. Today we understand that as right-brain dominance, and teachers now realize that there is a need to incorporate at least ten different learning modalities in order to teach and meet the individual needs of all students.

Like the God who tried to label me a sinner, the educational system also seemed unfair and uncaring. I resented and rejected being misjudged. At an early age, I learned to disregard the system, any system. And I was determined that my own children would experience a different understanding of learning.

At the termination of the school year, the children at my daughter's school brought home their classroom pictures. When my daughter showed me hers, I commented on the absolutely wonderful bone structure of the face of one of the boys in her class. Her reaction was, "Oh Nick, he's a Greek." My heart skipped a beat. I was floored by my daughter's response.

One thing that an international living accomplished was a sense of tolerance and acceptance. "He's a Greek." That statement and, more than anything, the way it was said, revealed a complete lack of respect for others. Such narrow-mindedness was against the very thing we attempted to instill in the lives of our children. Without saying a word to her, I called her father and informed him of the need to find a new school for the following year.

In time, the family reunited and we moved back to the Village in Manhattan. Our international lifestyle made us realize that our children would probably, one day in the future, encounter an alternative avenue to meet their educational needs. We knew that a boarding school might come into the picture, so we thought that we had better introduce them to a limited away-from-home experience, in case it did someday present itself.

While searching for a new school, we located a Summer Hill style summer camp in Claverack, New York. At Summer Hill children select classes based on interest. They develop at a pace which is completely individualistic.

Our children were a bit young to be separated from their parents, but we felt they would have each other, and if they weren't happy, they could quit summer school at any time.

We drove along the Hudson River to visit the camp. The director had started the school because he wanted an alternative educational experience for his own three boys. We met the teachers and children, who ranged in age from tots to teenagers. The atmosphere had a feeling of a large extended family. It felt right.

Our children were impressed and tickled by the school because they could have their own garden plot, help gather eggs from the hen house, and help care for the young cow. There were kids hugging the cow and gently sliding down her back. I had never seen a more contented animal. At feeding time, she ran up to food as if she were a puppy.

We enrolled them in the summer camp and, with a picnic basket in hand, visited them on weekends. They stayed until the last day and chose to return in the fall.

The full school year demanded a different schedule and another boarding school, with a different regime.

At eight o'clock on Monday mornings our children, Selena and Noah, boarded a van, along with a group of other city kids, to ride to upstate New York. We'd meet again in Union Square at five o'clock Friday evenings. They got to choose a restaurant, which usually meant eating crab in China Town. We'd return home and spend the next three nights together. Once in a while they stayed at school for the weekend because they didn't want to miss a special school activity or because we were traveling out of town.

In the spring, my husband was going on a business trip to South America and I decided to join him for the last week of his tour. The plan was to meet in Peru and continue on to Argentina and Brazil.

My plane arrived very early in the morning in Lima and I was ready for three days of fun. In the airport a sign announced the departure of a small aircraft to Cuzco and Machu Picchu, the lost city of the Incas. I checked my luggage into overnight storage, bought a ticket and hopped on the plane. In Cuzco, there was a small train that lurched around curves as it climbed the mountain to Machu Picchu. The seats were reserved. I sat next to a tall, young, American adult male, his two girl friends rested on a bench-like seat across from me.

Spending the night at the old Hotel Cuzco was a pleasant experience. The next morning I went to the bank to change money and, to my surprise, the American man was standing in line waiting for the bank to open. He signaled for me to come over. We made small talk and, after cashing money, went our separate ways.

At one o'clock I saw him again while I was in the airport ticket line. He came over and stood behind me. He was an antique dealer and saw that I didn't have luggage, so he wondered if I would check in one of his suitcases because he was going to be charged for an extra bag. I accommodated him and we boarded the plane. We sat next to each other.

It turned out that he was a very unhappy person because he had been robbed in Quito, Ecuador. In his lost billfold was a precious last letter from his dead wife. They had been madly in love, and she had died of cancer after giving birth to their first child. He had longed for her and couldn't get his life together without her until a North American Indian Shaman, who was over one hundred years old, sat with him in meditation to free and separate their spirits.

When the plane landed, we opened our luggage and exchanged books about gurus. He gave me an address where we could meet in case I needed help while in Lima. We parted and I set off to find a hotel. His experience with the Shaman was exciting and I secretly wished it would happen to me. Meeting him set me up for a situation that was about to take place, and I don't think I would have been free enough to dare to experience it if we hadn't met. This lesson opened me up to the idea that our lives are not made up of coincidences, but fateful choices.

After registering at a hotel and settling into my room, the next move was to locate a vegetarian restaurant that the hotel clerk had recommended. It was time for lunch, so I began a search for the restaurant. Thirty minutes later, I found what I was looking for.

Upon entering the eatery, I saw a sign that read "Meditation Tonight." I was pleased with the idea of having a chance to meet people from a foreign country who meditate. The owners of the restaurant turned out to be from Chile, rather than Peru, and talking to them was exciting because now I had a chance to meet more foreigners who were open to progressive practices.

As I entered the room at seven o' clock that evening, the room was empty. Soon a man came in and started to set up the chairs for the meeting. He recognized me as a foreigner and greeted me with, "Hello, sister. How are you enjoying my country?" My response was congenial, but I told him how disappointing it was not to be able to see relics like those I had seen at Cuzco. They had been few in number and tomorrow the museum in Lima, which is a good distance from town, would close early.

He said, "Oh, don't worry. The Inca Historian for Peru will be here tonight. I'm sure that he will take good care of you and show you whatever you want to see."

No sooner were those words spoken, when the door opened and in walked Joaquin, the Inca Historian.

The first gentleman introduced us and explained my dilemma. Joaquin replied, "There is a full moon Inca ceremony this evening. Would you like to attend?" He hesitated before he said, "You watch us during this gathering and then decide if you will join us."

Soon many young and older people entered the room for the meeting. When Joaquin stood up to address the audience, there was a wide white light surrounding his body. The white light was my sign that this would be a safe venture. He was, in my eyes, the equivalent of a younger Inca Shaman.

When the meeting ended, I agreed to attend what I thought was going to be a moonlight marriage. Informing Joaquin that I didn't have a gift for the bride and pointing to my earrings, I asked, "Will these do?" He laughed and gently said, "Oh, this isn't going to be a marriage ceremony."

Joaquin instructed me to go to my hotel, put on slacks, walking shoes, take a blanket from my bed (we were going to stay overnight), and bring whatever, if any, food I had. His parting words were, "We will pick you up in thirty minutes."

When they arrived, "we" turned out to be two men. I had imagined a group from the meeting would attend this affair. For a moment, I rethought my situation, remembered my complete faith in the White Light, and walked out of the door with cashew nuts, my gear, and two male strangers from a foreign country.

Our first stop was Joaquin's office, where we picked up a motion picture camera, a small regular camera, and a black suitcase. We walked to a crossroads in the center of Lima. There were lines of people standing on four corners. We got in line and waited. A car that was going in our direction stopped.

Joaquin talked to the driver, and we got in the back seat and left the city.

For over an hour we drove along dark, winding roads. This provided us time for a long talk. It turned out that Juan, the other man, had been fasting for seven days; I had been a vegetarian for seven months. Joaquin took this as a sign that we were preparing for an initiation.

"Seven," he said, "is a mystical number. It means realization."

When he learned that my birthday was on the twenty-fourth of June, which is an auspicious holiday in Peru, he was sure that I had been Inca in a past life.

He reiterated, "I believe that you have come to my country to be initiated. If you agree, please inform me when we arrive at the caves." Caves! I swallowed twice.

The car stopped, and Joaquin went to a small white house at the side of the road, knocked at the door, talked to a man, returned to the car, and talked to our driver. We got out of the car and started walking up a wide, rocky lama path. Joaquin asked each of us to carry something. The two men were huffing and puffing as they climbed up the mountain trail. I congratulated myself on being a vegetarian because I walked for over half an hour without stopping.

Finally, we arrived at the caves. They were small and, because of the full moon, you could see inside. There was only enough room for one body.

Joaquin found a flat clearing and put down a large blanket. He said again, "Do you want to be initiated?"

I answered, "Yes."

He placed me sitting up in one cave and Juan in another. One of us faced with feet out and the other with feet in. My instructions were to come out when the music began.

I waited for some time, so Juan must have been initiated first.

Upon hearing flute music, I came out, stood up and followed the sound. Seeing the two of them shook me up. Juan had on a blue Egyptian headdress and Joaquin wore identical robes to those I had seen on a Coptic Christian leader at a meeting in Michigan. An Egyptian influence in a ceremony in Peru, to me, was mind-boggling.

Joaquin approached me and placed a silver band with three sacred feathers on my head, and a cape of blue and gold bird feathers was placed on my shoulders. There had been a cape like this in the small museum in Cuzco. A sacred ceremony was performed and I was given an Inca name which means, "The Cleansing of the White Heart."

It was time to sleep, Joaquin laid out a large blanket for ground covering. He had me sleep fully dressed between the fully dressed two of them. We had our individual blankets to cover us.

At sunrise, we ate the food and re-enacted the scene of coming out of the caves for the movie camera.

That night, high in the Andes Mountains, under a carpet of stars and a full moon, I had to make a major decision about where spirituality was taking me. Joaquin said he could give me the names of people and book shops in Buenos Aires where I could find information about Inca ritual and ceremonies. When I arrived back in America, I would have had books and moving pictures.

Alex had once told me if you wanted, in spiritually, to go all the way to the White Light, you had to climb the ascending stairs of a pyramid of open doors. Each door invited you in. You could pause on your way to gain fame, riches, whatever you desired. The ground floor doors started with gold, sexuality, and intellect. Lifetime after lifetime gave you a new chance to choose a door or doors to enter. As you neared the top and got closer and closer to being successful, the enticements became more and more subtle.

29

I reviewed my situation and decided not to open the door Joaquin was offering.

The next morning, we walked down the mountain and waited for our driver to pick us up for the ride back to Lima.

Once in the car, Joaquin kept repeating, "You have been so brave." He explained that I had sent out a wonderful vibration for women of the world. An amazing invitation was extended to me because of the initiation: I was invited, anytime during my lifetime, to join the High Order of Inca Priests for their annual Andes procession on June twenty-fourth, my birthday. The White Light at the top of the pyramid kept me from ever going.

When we arrived at the hotel mid-morning, Juan and I smiled at each other and said, "Adiós!" Joaquin said he would see me later. I slept, and that evening Joaquin and his wife took me out to dinner. My husband arrived the next day.

Lesson Five - Meeting The Mother

In 1971, our family moved to Uganda, East Africa. My husband was the principal at Lincoln International School and I was one of six teachers. The school provided a lovely house with an extensive yard, located on Embassy Row. We had the use of a school minivan on weekends, so on various occasions we drove to one of the numerous game parks in the surrounding area, usually in Kenya. We were fortunate enough to encounter most of the wonderful wild animals that East Africa had to offer.

On one moonlit night, we slept in a cabin at the foot of Mount Kilimanjaro. The following week on a glorious Sunday afternoon, we toured the sweet freshwater Lake Victoria, observing the exotic Ugandan Crested Cranes. A month later, we rode in a handmade riverboat down the crocodile lined White Nile River. Our vacations included visiting Nairobi, Mombasa, Madagascar, Tanzania, and the historic tour of Ethiopia. Our life seemed as perfect as life could get.

One peaceful evening, a knock on our front door entirely changed our vision. The mother of an Israeli boy in my class wanted his report card. Their family, along with others, had been given twenty-four hours to leave the country. Those were the days of the notorious leader Idi Amin Dada. Politically, no one knew what to expect of him from one day to the next. My husband was Jewish. He quickly decided that we would leave Uganda at the termination of one, instead of two, school years.

During our stay, my search for the mysterious dark-eyed, dark-haired man continued. One room (more like a large closet) in our home was set aside as my meditation abode. Alex sent me tapes of his U.S. lectures, and I joined a local Indian study group who were followers of the Sikh, Guru Nanak.

An internal development was beginning. One day my physical body began an extreme change.

At intervals, perhaps weekly, while still in bed (so my husband could witness), a force like a pulsating cleaver would descend on the top of my head. This force would beat rhythmically at the same spot each time. It was as if it were slowly cracking my head open. There was always heat and tremendous pressure. I would silently sit on the edge of my bed with tears streaming down the sides of my face. When my head ached so much that I could no longer stand anymore of the quivering drilling, I would inwardly request the force to stop and it immediately obeyed.

At this, my husband remarked, "These are not normal headaches."

One evening, when the family was seated around the dining room table, another curious action occurred. Suddenly, almost violently, our nine year old son began to uncontrollably shake his head from side to side, as if he were saying, "No." This continued for what seemed like a minute and then it slowly subsided. My husband and I glanced at each other from across the table and said nothing.

At school the next day, we asked our son's teacher if he had witnessed this behavior in the classroom or out on the playground. He looked surprised, shrugged his shoulders and replied, "Never." The shaking of his head was like a no, no, no action. Inside of myself, I could have screamed. Why was a nine-year old child say saying "no, no, no!" What had we, his parents, done wrong to cause such dramatic disillusionment?

Within a moment, that inner voice came to me again. It said, "This is not for you. This is to show his father that this child needs a different type of education."

My reaction was to think, "Type? What on earth does that mean? Help! For God's sake, somebody please help me!" Perplexed and numb, I said nothing.

The following day, our family was invited to supper at the home of Saravanan, an Indian architect, and Marie-Ange, his lovely French wife.

After the meal was served, my husband and the hostess had coffee on the porch where they could speak French. Our children and their two children played outside. Saravanan and I were having our drinks in the den. During our conversation, we discussed what had happened to my son while we were at the table the night before. He observed my worried concern about not knowing how to deal with the situation. Very nonchalantly, he said, "Maybe you need to do what we did with our daughter, Shivani."

Saravanan explained how very happy she was at an excellent English-speaking boarding school that was directed by a woman called the Mother. The school was located at the Sri Aurobindo Ashram in southern India.

Saravanan and Marie-Ange had decided to send Shivani to a boarding school because she was nervous, biting her nails and crying every time they, her parents, got into a heated argument.

My question to this explanation was, "Who is The Mother?"

Saravanan pointed to a bookcase with thirteen volumes of white leather-bound books. He smiled, gestured with open hands, and said, "These are all about the Mother."

Saravanan advised me to take a book home. I informed him that I didn't have time to read because we were preparing for the end of the school year and our trip home.

My husband and I wondered about the possibility of the value of this school for our children. We thought about it for some time and then decided he would fly home with them and I would go to India to check out the school.

When it was time to leave Africa, Saravanan had heard that I was going to Pondicherry to visit the school of the Mother. He decided to join me because he hadn't seen Shivani for some time.

On the airplane flight we talked about the spiritual leaders who led the Ashram. The French woman, "the Mother," was born and educated in France. The man, Sri Aurobindo, was born in India and educated in England at St Paul's School in London and, later, at Cambridge University. Saravanan was a devotee of the Mother. He opened his wallet and showed me Her picture.

Attending an Ashram was a new experience for me. When we arrived in Pondicherry, I followed my friend from place to place. He registered me into the Ashram's Park Guest House and then we went to the Ashram dining room for a silent evening meal. Later, while he went to find his daughter, I walked along the sea back to my room. While seated in the lobby talking to some Ashramites, Saravanan rushed in. He was so excited. He kept repeating, "Shirley, we have an appointment with the Mother!"

Trying not to show it, I must have disappointed my friend greatly because of my lack of enthusiasm for his good news. I wasn't interested in meeting this lady. I just wanted to see the school. Looking back, it was my lucky day, but I was too blasé to realize it then.

An appointment with the Mother was very special because She was now older and could not carry on with all She had once done. Even the school children were no longer able to visit Her on their birthdays. The only reason we had the good fortune of meeting the Mother was because of a woman who was acting as a big sister to Saravanan's daughter and she was one of the Mother's closest secretaries. She had asked permission and the Mother had honored her request. I was given specific instructions to sit at the top of the stairs outside of the Mother's room at eleven in the morning, with a flower in my hand. I thought, "A flower? Why and what flower?"

Saravanan walked me over to the flower shop, which was just across the courtyard from the stairs to the Mother's room. He told me, "If you don't know what flower to give Her, the attendant in the shop will automatically pick the right one." The Mother had renamed all the flowers. Rather than speak to Her, you handed Her a flower which would express your message to Her. Her answer would be in the name of the flower She gave back to you.

Upon my return to the lobby of the guest house, a man greeted me saying, "I heard you are going to see the Mother. Let me show you the garden we have made for Her."

We walked a short distance and entered an area which contained a variety of beautiful flowers. He proceeded to name many of them, using words like Devotion, Aspiration, Beauty, and Truth. He informed me that the next morning he would cut any flower I desired. I thanked him for his assistance and let him know I was going to let the flower shop choose the right one for me.

At ten o'clock the next morning, I went to the flower shop and explained my need for a flower. With surprise, the attendant exclaimed, "The flowers don't come in until twelve o'clock. No one sees the Mother at this time. This must be special."

He looked around and said, "I have one flower left from yesterday." As he handed me the flower, he continued, "This delicate flower must be what you are looking for. It means Intimate Relationship."

I looked at him, thanked him, bit my nails, and, with this fragile flower in hand, jumped on my Ashram bike. I peddled it as fast as it could take me back to the guest house garden. Luckily, the gentleman from the night before was tending the flowers and he anticipated my need. He reiterated, "The garden is yours."

I marched over, pointed to a flower (thinking I had remembered its name), and asked him to please cut a large bud, one that was just opening. He cut the flower and said, "You know what you chose, don't you?"

I confidently replied, "Yes, Psychological Perfection." Inside my head I thought, "That will put a good distance between me and Intimate Relationship."

He laughed and said, "Oh, no, you picked Surrender."

I gulped, put the two flowers together, the one from the shop and now the garden, and made the comment, "I'm a watercolor painter of flowers. Do you think we could make this a bit more artistic?"

He lovingly cut seven small reddish-pink roses from the garden, arranged them around the two flowers in my hands, and sent me on my way. I hurried back to the Ashram and quietly walked up the stairs to sit on the landing in front of the Mother's room.

A short time later, Saravanan reeled out of the door in front of me. The silence of the day was abruptly shaken. He was uncontrollably sobbing and threw himself down on the top stair.

I said to myself, "My word, who is this lady? I guess I'm next!"

I cautiously entered the open door of a large room that was very bright because of its huge, wide windows. Seated on my left was a bent-over figure of an elderly woman. She was alone, and on the left side of Her was a huge pot of flowers

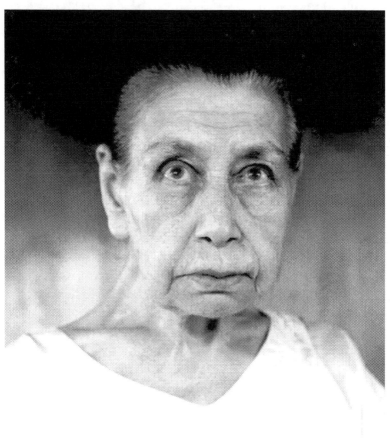

THE GAZE OF THE MOTHER

The only way to look into Her eyes was to place myself, on bended knees, at Her feet. With a reverent bow, I offered (handed) Her my flowers. As I did so, She looked directly into my eyes and suddenly Her eyes became huge. Her eyes seemed twice their size. With a strong, steady stare, She poured Her tremendous energy into me. I felt it curl (twirl), as it dug below the pit of my stomach. A coil of a dirty, negative feeling sprung from the depth of my being.

I thought, "Oh my God. Is that who I am? I'm embarrassed. She can see inside of me!"

From the first moment of our encounter, because of what the Mother was seeing, She seemed to have a look of shock on Her face. She stared with a steady force until I now realize She uprooted something in me. Then She softened Her gaze, smiled a loving smile, and reached for a flower. As She handed me a salmon-colored rose, an electric shock slowly vibrated up and down my right arm. I felt She was charging me. Numb, I smiled reverently, bowed again, and left the room. I slowly descended the stairs and seated myself in front of the Samadhi.

The Samadhi is an enclosed courtyard. In the center is a rectangular tomb encasing the body of Sri Aurobindo, and now, the Mother too. Daily, devotees sit in silence while others decorate the area above the tomb with designs made from petals of flowers. It is the major devotional center of the Ashram.

The following day, I was to board an airplane home, so I decided I should buy a book to read about this lady, the Mother. I wandered into an Ashram bookstore. Once inside, I could hardly believe my eyes. There on the wall were two, side by side, gigantic portraits of the gurus. One was the woman, the Mother, whom I had just seen, and the other was the exact photo of those intense dark eyes, dark hair and that white wire-like beard. The mysterious man who had come to me in a vision four years earlier in Barcelona, was none other than Sri Aurobindo.

Inwardly, I rejoiced. Outwardly, I stood in front of Them transfixed. After four years of looking, here He was, my mysterious man! He, indeed, was a real person and not a figment of my imagination!

The date below His picture informed me that He had left His body on December 5, 1950. Seventeen years later, He had come to me on July 7, 1967. Wow! Once again, I had to readjust my head, my thinking. I asked myself, "How is it possible that a ghost could appear seventeen years after He left his body?"

Flabbergasted, I was suddenly aware of how little I knew about life. I felt happy and more than justified, not because I needed reassurance, since I was absolutely sure what I had experienced that morning in Barcelona was true. But now there was positive proof to show my dubious family and friends that the man I had been searching for really did exist.

Instantly, upon realizing how privileged I had been because of having personal moments with two dynamic human beings, my heart asked, "Why me? What on earth do They want of insignificant me?"

Little did I realize that on that day, while on my knees in front of the Mother, something deep and unknown inside of me surrendered to Her. I half remember thinking, but not saying, "If you need a human instrument on this planet to help you with your mission, I offer myself." Inside of my head She answered, "I can't use you if you are emotional." Later, a few years later, I kept asking, while completely mystified, why I had imagined such a thing.

Now, because of our relationship, I know the answer. I needed to serve Her.

In 1972 She had Written:

*"For centuries humanity has waited for this time. It is come.
But it is difficult. I don't simply tell you we are here upon
earth to rest and enjoy ourselves, now is not the time for that.
We are here to prepare the way for the New Creation."*

The Mother: Notes on the Way, p. 3

Lesson Six – =1

When it was time to leave India I stepped onto the airplane in Madras to return to my family. My destination was Mexico. My husband had decided to start an alternative educational program to provide a culturally diverse experience for junior and senior high school students. The students would receive high school credit for attending a three-month course called Educational Opportunities Abroad (EOA). The program would include: Spanish language, history, art, cooking, dancing lessons, and field trips in and around Mexico, mostly in Monterrey.

The issue in the forefront of my mind was the fact that I had been told that our son needed a different type of education, and I certainly had been shown something new. I placed the recent experience of the school in India before myself, as a part of what might be right for him, but now I was also interested in returning to Pondicherry.

September came and together with the children we were getting ready to travel to India. Just before we purchased the tickets, my daughter asked me if the people in India were as poor as the people in Ethiopia. I answered, "Not all of them are poor but, yes, most of them live like they do in Ethiopia."

My daughter lowered her eyes and said, "It hurts my heart to see anyone live like that. I don't want to go there."

Believing that I needed this experience for her brother, and now for myself, I asked her what she would like to do if she didn't come with us. She decided to stay with her father and attend an International School in Mexico. She was fluent in Spanish, so we didn't think it would be difficult for her to adjust. We enrolled her in a school and bought schoolbooks and uniforms. Her brother and I delayed our trip to make sure that she had made the right decision. She hadn't.

Two weeks later, she didn't like the classes, but she still didn't want to go with us. We had to change direction and we had to change fast.

Plan A had been to have her come to India with us. Plan B had her going to school in Mexico and living with her father. Now Plan C put her in school in America, where she could be near her cousins and stay with her grandmother, my mother. I thought that my mother had her life back under control, so my husband took my daughter to Michigan while I took our son to India. I intended to visit her as soon as I returned, with or without her brother.

When our plane arrived at the terminal in Madras, I hired a taxi driver who brought along a male friend to help drive us three hours south to Pondicherry. It turned out to be a nightmarish ride. I was so happy that my son slept most of the way. I kept asking myself what madness I had placed before us because there were potholes everywhere and we bounced around in the back seat the whole time.

As we arrived in Pondicherry, I had the driver take us to the same Ashram guest house that I had stayed in at the time I was there with Saravanan. We lived in a comfortable, but modest, room and ate at the Ashram dining room. Since they didn't serve meat, we frequently ate in a local restaurant because I felt that my son's body was accustomed to having more protein.

A shattering shock hit me when I went to enroll my son in classes. There was a one-year waiting list for new students!

I had been so absorbed in my experience with the Mother and Sri Aurobindo that I had forgotten to check out the admissions policy. I did ask Shivani and her friends about the quality of the classes and had talked to some teachers, but it never entered my mind that there would not be room in the school for a new student.

There were many Americans and Europeans at the Ashram, and they had formed another school to accommodate the overflow of the Ashram school. It was called =1.

Academically, the curriculum was centered on the philosophy of a French woman, Yvonne. Incorporated in the learning methodology was the Jungian idea of a sandbox designed for the use of children of all ages. The area of the sandbox was about 3 ft. by 5 ft., and it stood almost as high as a standard table. On many shelves along the wall were toys from all over the world.

The method of the sandbox was that a child would plan and execute a design in the entire area of the sandbox. The teacher would then sketch a picture of the sandbox and file it in the child's folder. Each child would then clear the sandbox as they returned all the toys back on the shelves.

At the parent/teacher conference, there wasn't a verbal explanation of the work, just a file of pictures. The idea was to watch the growth of a child as he/she tried to center themselves.

When my young son, Noah, arranged his first sandbox, he was the buzz of the teacher's lounge. He had made a long line of cars, buses, trains, horses, camels, and people going to visit the Sphinx.

Once the school situation was out of the way, we turned our attention to finding a place to live. We found a small Ashram house that was for rent along the Bay of Bengal. The house had a lovely upstairs terrace overlooking the water. We could watch the fishermen in their boats and stand on the beach when they brought in the catch of the day. It was a thrill to watch them open their nets. A crowd of women would be waiting to buy food to sell or prepare for their evening meal.

To help Noah get around, I rented him a bike. He informed me seven dollars a month was a rip-off. I told him that when he knew for certain that he wanted to stay and go to school there, I would buy him a bike. He never asked me to buy one. That was my first clue that he didn't want to stay in India.

Every new child at the Ashram had a meeting with the Mother, which was something special, as She was not meeting people anymore. When Noah's turn came, we were both very excited. He showered and had to decide what to wear for this wonderful occasion. I placed on the bed three clean outfits for him to choose from: his play clothes, a tailored India gray suit from Uganda, and a new white tennis shirt and shorts. He chose white, without realizing it was the perfect color for a visit to the Mother.

Gene, an adult American friend, escorted Noah to meet with Her. When they returned, we walked along the sea. Noah couldn't keep his feet on the ground. He danced and pranced as he sang, "Now I'm free. You can't tell me anymore what to do or what to wear because I'm free. I'm going to see Her every week!"

I told him that he was lucky to have seen Her once and, for the moment, he should be content with that. As I rethought about the meeting, I wondered if the Mother had aroused something deep, deep within his being.

As I walked around the Ashram, dark, round, red scars were noticeable on the bodies of some Westerners. When I inquired about the reason for the scars, various people explained that they thought they were from the cleansing of blood that was the result of a one-on-one meeting each person had with the Mother. These scars came from boils that would eventually disappear. Noah got boils.

The next day, about ten o'clock in the morning, I walked past the health clinic and Noah was seated inside next to an elderly male Ashramite.

I stepped in and asked, "What are you doing here?" Noah raised his bandaged foot as if to say, "This."

The man replied, "He had a boil on the bottom of his foot and it is taken care of."

The gentleman shooed me away, saying, "Go have a nice cup of tea. The children in this Ashram are the responsibility of all of us."

Noah met me later. He hadn't told me about the boil and since he walked on foam flip-flops, I hadn't noticed it. At the school, you take off your shoes. That was how they saw him limp. Noah never complained, but slowly was deciding not to stay.

When Noah knew for sure that he did not want to remain in India, he refused to leave until he saw the Mother again, for one last time. I was told that in order for him to see Her, he would have to write a note and ask for Her permission. He did so and She said yes.

One eventful day, at one o'clock P.M., we went to see Her. We stood in a long line with many others. I told my son if he really wanted to see the Mother, know who She was, he had to look directly into Her eyes. As we approached Her, he got down on his knees and gazed up. He took his own sweet time. Then he rose. I bowed slightly and we moved on.

There was a goodbye party for Noah at the school, but he was so sick after seeing the Mother, that he couldn't attend his own party. I wondered if this was another cleansing. Noah sat on a curb outside the school, vomiting until he had the dry heaves. An hour later, he sipped a cup of tea.

Before we left the Ashram for good, Noah had a dream that his bicycle chain had snapped. He couldn't fix it and couldn't ride his bike. When he looked down, he saw that on one foot he had on an American sneaker and on the other an Indian slipper.

Later I explained the dream to Yvonne, the head mistress. When I told her that I thought the meaning of the dream was that he could not decide whether to follow an American or an Indian way of life, she said, "No. I believe he can't decide whether to follow his inner or outer self."

Lesson Seven – The Packet

The first month after our arrival in India, I had heard some curious stories about why some people had come to live at the Ashram. I thought the most interesting story was told by an Irishman from Boston named John.

In World War II, he was a Sergeant in the United States Army and was on active duty during the invasion of Germany. He and a group of his men were cornered in a small farmhouse. Some German soldiers were within shooting distance and the Irishman had the responsibility of getting his men out of the house safely. He couldn't figure out how to accomplish this.

As he smoked a cigarette, the smoke rose up and started to form the upper part of a man's body. This ghost-like man unexpectedly said to him, "Each time the Germans fire a round of shots, send one of your men outside to the clump of trees."

Inside the house, John kept walking around in circles not knowing what to believe. He went to the bathroom and sat on the toilet. He lit another cigarette, and the smoke formed the upper body of the same man. This time the ghost-man said, "Why aren't you doing what I told you to do?"

So John followed His directions and safely got all of his men out of the house.

Years later, while walking past a bookstore, John saw in the window, on the cover of a book, a photo of the smoky ghost-man. He went in and bought the book, and discovered Sri Aurobindo. It was the same picture of the mysterious ghost visitor who had come to me in Barcelona. John sold all of his things in America and moved to the Ashram to live out the rest of his life.

John told me this story while we were sitting in an Indian coffee house in Pondy.

The following event was just as mysterious. While in bed having a very restless time trying to fall asleep, I tossed and turned for an hour or so. Unexpectedly and speedily, my consciousness rose to a patch of blue above my head. The intense, clear color was wide and expansive. A man's voice (intuitively I knew it was Sri Aurobindo) said, "That is the only ability available to your mind."

With a sense of great confusion, I came back down to my bed.

That statement had me perplexed for many years. I now believe that the only ability available to our mind is to use the mind to go step-by-step beyond the mind.

The next experience has to do with the Mother and Darshan Day.

On this day, the Mother came out of Her room onto Her balcony to give Her blessing. The street in front of Her house was lined with Ashramites and guests. They stood twenty feet deep. While standing on the wide street in front of Her and not knowing what to expect, the Mother slowly began looking over the crowd. Starting to the left of me, at the beginning of the line which was over a city block long, She gave each section of people the advantage of a direct, steady stare.

As She approached our area, you could feel Her force coming near. When She looked directly in front of us, Her gaze made me feel as though every cell in my body had turned into pudding. A stream rippled throughout my being. The Mother stood in silence. None moved or made a sound. The crowd watched this small, slender body of an elderly woman as She revealed the power of a dynamic force. Once you had witnessed that energy, you never doubted why She had come to bring Her Light to this planet.

As I left the scene, I knew I would never view life in the same way. I now understood why multitudes of people followed Jesus. It just takes one look.

The most profound event, for me, happened one month after we were in Pondy.

The mother of my son's friend asked if Noah could stay at her house for a week. There were many friends coming to visit her two children and they were going to have a week full of spontaneous fun. She didn't want Noah to miss it. Her house was ten blocks from my house, so it would be easy for the children to come and see me during that week. Little did I know that I desperately needed a week by myself. Later, I reflected that the Mother must have arranged this free time, so She could uninterruptedly work on me.

Soon after they left, while listening to Indian music, I had a very deep meditation. A force came down through my head to my navel area. I felt ill.

That evening I had an etheric experience of seeing four gigantic pictures. They were as large as a movie screen. Each picture was in color and depicted an aspect of disgusting human habits. During the viewing of one of the pictures, I had to turn my face from the scene because the odor was putrid.

The next day, I began to vomit, it was impossible to hold food in my stomach. There was no reason to go to the health clinic because there wasn't a sign of fever or any other symptoms of being ill.

After four days of only drinking tea, I thought that I would force myself to eat because I had no energy left and was just lying around in the house. I got on my bike and cycled to the European Ashram tearoom. It was around two or three o'clock in the afternoon.

While sitting alone in silence and eating a bowl of rice with yogurt, the food didn't settle well. Racing home on my bicycle, I got into my yard just in time. Suddenly it felt as if someone had turned a hose on inside of me. With great force, the food came shooting out of my mouth. I went to bed and realized that I shouldn't have had anything more than tea.

At dawn the next morning, I was sleeping on my stomach. Abruptly, and very deep inside of me, it felt as though an explosion had taken place. It seemed like slivers of glass were stuck in my fingers. The glass at my fingertips had the feeling of being thin, an inch wide and three inches long, with a spear-like point. There also seemed to be a huge square of glass about ten or twelve inches wide and two inches thick, with a triangular point stuck in my back. I felt that if someone would pull the spears of glass out of my fingers, blood would uncontrollably gush out. I had to decide to cry out for help or shout, "Take it out!" I yelled, "Take it out!"

With the release of those words, a tremendous, directed force pulled the piece of glass out of my back. Along with the glass, it pulled out a fighting, resisting, human shaped body. The body wasn't skin and bones. It was a concentrated cloud of vapors.

I was lying on my stomach, so I just felt it go. I felt nauseated, upset with myself that such a negative, ugly, feeling thing could have been inside of me. I then remembered the first time I met the Mother and the shock in Her eyes when She forced the coil in the depths of me to unfurl. This ugly thing was what She must have seen. I felt like I was a container in which both of us lived, me along with this ugly visitor that had just been pulled out.

Recalling my near-death experience when I was a child, I wondered if my consciousness had been so weak that I hadn't been strong enough to fight back a being that wanted to possess me. I felt sure this was a male being. When I came back to my senses, I had a good laugh because if that were the case, he sure got a bum deal to have chosen a Dutch Reformed religious goody-goody like me. I bet it was a constant frustration.

I got up, showered, and went to have breakfast, rice and milk. All day long, I walked around the Ashram, in and out of places, not being able to shake the feeling of the large hole in my back.

By the second day, that feeling was still wide open. I was working at the educational center and told the director, Norman Dowsett, what had happened. He said, "You must write and tell the Mother about this. That could be an evil force."

I composed a very short note on a sheet of insignificant notebook paper, enclosed it in an envelope, and took it to the office of Nolinida, one of the Mother's secretaries.

The next day, while seated on the porch reading, Shivani came hurriedly on her bicycle into my yard. Before she could put down the bicycle, she yelled, "Shirley, you must come to pick up your mail. Your name is on the board that informs everyone they have correspondence from the Mother. Your name is printed in large, red capital letters. I have never seen that before, hurry!"

I went to Nolinida's office as quickly as possible. When I entered, he was seated at his desk. Nolinida looked up, smiled, and asked me my name. After telling him, he opened a large, folder-sized, red envelope and took out the little note. The note was in the same small envelope I'd sent to the Mother. He handed it to me. I put my hands together reverently, bowed slightly to express thank you, and left the room.

I sat just outside of his door in the Mother's meditation room and opened the envelope. Inside was the same note that I had written, nothing added, no comments from Her. I was so disappointed.

On further inspection, I found a lovely folded packet. The kind of flower packet you receive on the Mother's birthday or Darshan. This packet, however, was special. There was a thin, gold frame around the smiling picture of the Mother and inside in red letters written in Her handwriting was the date.

I went back in to see Nolinida. He smiled when I said, "I don't understand."

He said, as he made namaste with hands together, "You will, you will." Somewhat frustrated, I returned his bow, smiled and left the room.

Three months had passed and it was time to leave the Ashram. Noah had not asked me to buy him a bike and he was ready to return home. I hadn't seen my daughter for such a long time. We anxiously boarded the plane for Mexico. When we arrived, my son stayed there to live with his father. The start up of the new school EOA (Educational Opportunities Abroad) was not going well. There weren't enough students signed up for the first term. We were about to lose our entire investment, so to drum up more business, against my will and without time or money for a ticket to see my dear daughter in Michigan, I began working.

I had to move to Miami Beach to lecture about the program. I was sad not to be with my daughter and confused after what had happened to me in India. A body being pulled out of you isn't an everyday occurrence. Finances were tight. I couldn't even fly to my brother-in-law's house for the funeral of my sweet, loving mother-in-law.

When I arrived in Miami, my husband's friends who met my airplane gave me some information about an Ashram in Miami Beach. The following day, I went to a real estate agent and asked for a place to rent within ten city blocks of the location of the Ashram. The agent had never heard of the Ashram. That wasn't surprising because it turned out to be a small house with a closed-in yard, and wasn't really noticeable from the street. He checked the area and there was nothing for rent.

As I walked toward the Ashram address, I saw a man putting up a "For Rent" sign on a small cottage located on the canal. I moved in that afternoon.

At seven o'clock that evening, I was knocking on the Ashram door. The young man who answered would not allow me in because it was the seventh day of a ten-day India festival. I was invited to come the following morning at nine o'clock to attend a yoga class and meet the guru.

The next morning was Saturday, so I was free to join the group. As Shivananda Valentina, the guru, checked out my aura, she invited me to join them for the rest of the festival.

Other than the Mother, Shivananda Valentina was the first female guru I had met and it was a new approach to yoga.

Some days later, as a special gift to each of us, she allowed us to place an object that we wanted cleansed of its vibrations on a gold lacquered tray. A day later we could pick up the item from her inner chamber.

I had placed a ring on the tray and when I went to collect it, I found the tray below a huge, hanging poster-sized picture of Sri Aurobindo. I then realized why I was at this Ashram with this guru.

A few months later, while sitting in the meditation room of the Ashram, a young lady tapped me on the shoulder and informed me that the Mother in India had left Her body. I was numb. I didn't weep, just sat there motionless.

On two occasions the Mother had profoundly changed my life, and I would never be the same person that I had been before our encounters. We had recently met and now, without knowing enough about Her, She was gone forever. I thought that She was gone forever. Little did I realize what the future would hold.

Lesson Eight – Seven Screams

L ife was moving so fast. Things were better because our daughter had come to stay with me in Miami Beach. EOA did get enough students so there would be a group to leave for Mexico. Our daughter was too young to join the juniors and seniors in the summer program, but her parents owned the school, need I say more? Her impeccable use of Spanish would help conversations with the older students, so along with them she studied Mexican history, visited art galleries, danced and cooked.

One day while working on an art project, a very knowledgeable high school senior who my daughter greatly admired, stopped to watch her work. This student noticed a book about the famous Indian teacher, Krishnamurti, on the ground near her supplies. In an amazed voice, she asked my daughter if she was reading that book. Selena replied, "Oh my mother wants me to look that book over to see if I would like to attend his boarding school, Brockwood Park, in England." Selena further explained that she didn't think that she was interested in the school.

The high school student sighed, "Are you crazy? I would have given anything if my parents had made me this offer." Selena enrolled in Brockwood Park that fall.

While my husband and daughter attended the first EOA session, my son and I returned to Michigan to live with my mother. I had work lined up with a summer migrant program, but classes didn't begin for a few weeks. SFF was having a week-long conference, and my mother offered to take care of my son. The program began on Saturday. I eagerly arrived early on Friday evening because I wanted to be rested and ready for the next day.

Jim Goure, a retired naval officer who had a center called United Research in Black Mountain, North Carolina, was our leader for the conference. I didn't know anything about him or any other person who would attend. Jim was holding a meditation on Friday evening for those who had come early. The conference began the following day. I went to the meditation room and joined around thirty-five people. Jim welcomed us and told us about some of the upcoming events.

He then led us in a silent meditation. When we got up to leave the room, he came over to me and said, "A female being over a mile long came to this meeting tonight because of you." I looked at him with complete surprise and said nothing. My immediate reaction was, "it must be the Mother." Ever since that first meeting when I gave Her the flower "Surrender," I intuitively knew that we were connected and my responsibility to Her was to sit in silence and let Her light descend through me to ground Her force wherever I went. Without understanding why, I had meditated and done that in airports and churches around the world.

Before school ended, my daughter, Selena, had called me from Brockwood Park. She asked if we could follow the Krishnamurti crowd to Switzerland to attend the yearly K (Krishnamurti) talks which would be held during the first week in June. Some of her teachers and friends would be there and she wanted to join them. A special time alone with my daughter was just what I had been waiting for. I eagerly agreed to her plan.

A week before the meeting in Switzerland, there was a three-day retreat with Alex. He had taken me on as his student and sent me tapes of his lectures the entire time we lived in Africa. I was looking forward to an intense cleansing workshop with him and a sadhu from India. Once again, I arrived early. He picked me up at the airport on Thursday evening and took me to a meeting of his devotees. I was pleased because I felt it was a special treat to be included in this small intimate group.

We sat together, listening to the evening lecture. Without warning, the guru stood up, came over to where I was seated, and placed his forehead on my forehead. After a short period of time, he softly whispered to me, "I have married you on the other side." I said nothing because we were in front of all of his students, but I was shocked, embarrassed and upset. My immediate reaction was, "What is this? How dare you?" He had not asked my permission to marry me. Didn't I have a say in this transaction? We were both married and what was he talking about when he mentioned the other side? Where is the other side? The whole scene was uncomfortable.

After the meeting, I rode back to my hotel with a young woman devotee who was going to be my roommate during the conference. She had observed what had happened and noticed my puzzled reaction. She explained that forehead to forehead was his version of new age sex. We went to our room to get ready for bed and as I undressed to put on my sleeping gown, she pointed to an area just above my bra. She said, "I'm a nurse and I see you have shingles." I looked down to see a bright red spot with tiny blisters. I was utterly surprised because there had been nothing there as I got dressed that morning. I asked her what caused shingles and she said, "Nerves."

That night, in the midst of a sound sleep, I was awakened by the voice of the Mother. She said, through me, to the guru at home in his own bed, "You male chauvinist!" I could have crawled under the bed! We had known each other for years and he had always been so kind to me. I never would have talked to him that way. But the Mother, in few words, expressed Her view. She was blunt and to the point. I could do nothing but live with the situation. Hiding from him the next day wasn't easy. Each time he came toward me, I shot off in another direction so his eyes wouldn't meet mine. Later that evening, he came over and said, "You handled that very well."

The intense workshop was just that, intense. There were constant lectures. It seemed everyone was pouring all their energy into clearing out old vibrations. During one of the meditations, the guru was performing a ceremony with the flicking of peacock feathers. As he flicked the feathers above my head, I felt a force moving up from the lower chakra (energy center). As this movement climbed up my spine, I let out a scream and as it touched each remaining chakra, I kept squealing. In the beginning, the screams were slight and somewhat controlled, but as it neared the top of my spine, the screams were much louder with a chilling effect.

I was sitting in a large room full of people and really didn't care what anyone else thought. I had come to make a big change in my life and if screaming was a part of it, in this case, so be it! When my body demanded a release, I fulfilled the body's request. There are seven chakras and I think I let out seven screams. It felt as if I were like a snake or a turtle that was breaking loose from my outer shell. I knew that I had shed something. Later, a man came up to me and said, "This is my first conference and when you screamed, I wanted to run out of the door."

During this retreat, if anyone had walked out of the door, they would have seen people sitting alone all over the fields.

Some were under trees crying and shaking. The object was to release past lifetime vibrations and most people were working hard to obtain their goal. In the late afternoon, while sitting alone, the guru came up to me and said, "You have done enough for this weekend."

I answered, "No, I really want to cleanse myself."

He said, "Woman, you have changed your cells, you have a whole new nervous system, enough is enough! Give yourself a rest." I got up and went back to my room to sleep. As I left the conference, I felt higher than a kite, renewed, very happy because of accomplishing my goal.

Returning to Michigan left me with one week before the migrant program began, so I flew to England to join my daughter for our upcoming exciting trip to Switzerland. Some of the Brockwood Park crew had left England early, so they were there when we arrived in Saanen. We were invited to join them for a one-day trip high in the Alps. We drove as high as we could go in a Land Rover and then we climbed over fields and rocks in order to get to the summer barn, where we ate raclette cheese melted over an open fire. My daughter and I felt that we were reliving the story of Heidi.

At the K (Krishnamurti) program, we camped along the side of a mountain stream with a group of other mothers and daughters. There were people everywhere. The schoolhouse had been turned into a large hostel, and students with sleeping bags had gathered all over the floor. We all lined up to eat our meals at the vegetarian food tent.

Each morning we went to hear K speak and spent the rest of the day individually contemplating what he had said. About three days into the talks, it started to rain, so a group of us women, with our daughters, rented a chalet. While we were inside the house, we sometimes ran around half-dressed.

One morning, a mother of one of the girls came up to me and said, "You have M, the initial of your name, on your breast above your bra." I looked in the mirror and there where the shingles had been was a red scar in the form of a large capital M. She was right, that was the beginning letter of my married name, but I quickly realized that the M represented the Mother. That letter M by the use of shingles was the Mother's way of telling me that She, at the retreat in Illinois, was responsible for the changing of my nervous system. One month later, I walked into a creative, new-age specialty workshop. A young woman artist came up to me and out of nowhere said, "You have the cells of the Mother."

Lesson Nine – The Third Eye

Both of our children were now at private schools. Our daughter was at Brockwood Park in England and our son was at a school in America. His school was near his cousins and grandparents, so he could come home weekends if he chose to do so. During the summers, my husband ran EOA and I returned to Michigan to be with my mother and work the migrant program. He returned to part-time work at his previous employment, which was setting up educational facilities for American companies around the world. Our home base was in New Brunswick, New Jersey. We had part time jobs and part-time lives. Yearly the company that employed my husband paid for the wife or husband to accompany their spouse on an educational conference anywhere in the world. I would choose the one that was the greatest distance from home, so I could stop and see many countries along the way. Our next conference was in Malaysia, so I flew there with him.

That year, there were two conferences in the same part of the world. When the first conference ended and before the next one began, we had a free weekend. We flew to the Ashram in Pondicherry. My husband was curious about where his son and I had lived for three months. Three days was more than enough time for him. He soon left to check on a school and I was to meet him in Egypt.

It was so exciting to be back in the Ashram atmosphere. Things were different because the Mother had left Her body, and the place was having a difficult time adjusting to life without Her. Nolinida, the one person I had hoped to see, was still there. As one of Her secretaries, he had handed me my letter from Her in the big red folder and his presence had touched my soul. He had a loving, smiling face. I had been so taken with him, and couldn't figure out why. For no logical reason, I wanted to give him a special gift. After racking my brain as to what would be proper to buy a man who had given up all worldly goods, the final choice was a steel manicuring set. It was in a small leather case.

To give him something presented an awkward situation because I didn't know if he remembered who I was. My inner feelings took over. I summoned up my courage and walked to his office. The door was shut. I thought, "Oh well, I guess I'm not supposed to give him anything." From behind me, Nolinida was shuffling up the path with his secretary at his side. Handing him the small gift, I said, "I feel the need to give you something."

He smiled his endearing smile, looked up at me, and said, "What is your name?"

I answered, "Shirley." He smiled again and went on his way.

I sat outside his room in the Mother's meditation area. A short while later, his secretary tapped me on the shoulder and said, "When he opened your gift he said, 'Very nice, very nice.' He never says anything when someone gives him something, so I wanted you to know."

That night, in the middle of my sleep, a huge, bright ball of light awakened me. It zoomed in and zoomed out of sight. I intuitively knew it was Nolinida.

Two days later, I saw an announcement on the Bulletin Board. Nolinida was giving a lecture in the high school gym. I wasn't an Ashramite, so I had to get special permission to attend. I arrived twenty minutes early and saw a crowded room of over two hundred people, dressed in white, sitting on the floor. Nolinida and his secretary were on the floor in front of the crowd. Hesitating as I stood in the doorway, I saw him talk to his secretary and she motioned for me to come and sit in front of them. I was surprised and wasn't sure they meant me. I looked around and saw that I was the only one standing in the doorway, so I assumed that it really was me. I walked to the front of the room, and the people in the first row squeezed together so I could sit down. As I neared Nolinida, he put his hands together and bowed twice. I bowed back. It looked like he had tears in his eyes. Maybe they were the eyes of an older man and not tears. They looked like tears to me. I left the next day and never saw him again.

There were four free days before I was to meet my husband in Egypt, so I flew to New Delhi for an overnight before I went to Kathmandu. In the late afternoon, while standing in a square in the tourist area of the city, a strange man appeared from out of nowhere. He plopped a large lump of white cream on my shoe, pointed up to the sky, and said, "A bird, a bird." Before I realized what was happening, he grabbed my new, expensive walking sandal and ran off. I stood there, perplexed, with one shoe on and one shoe gone.

Five minutes later, he returned with the white cream rubbed all over the shoe and with nails hammered into the sole. He said, "It was broken and I fixed it for you." He wanted to be paid for fixing it. Throwing my hands in the air, I walked away thinking, "These are my favorite shoes. I need them for the rest of my trip. They are new and certainly didn't need to be fixed. Now one shoe is dark and the other light!" I shook my head in disbelief and went on my way searching for a souvenir shop.

I was going to buy a sitar, sandalwood chess set, silk, and some semi-precious gems. I entered a nice looking shop and spent a lot of time looking at things. A rather young man (thirty-five), who owned the store, saw that I wasn't satisfied with some of his goods. He asked if I wanted to go to his warehouse, where he had many more items to choose from. It was getting late and I was leaving the next morning, so he drove me to his warehouse.

After I had selected all of the things to buy and had paid for them, he offered me a drink. We sat at a small table across from each other having something like a Tom Collins. After consuming more than half of the drink, I looked at him and there in the middle of his forehead was a large eye. A huge, normal looking eye! My mouth blurted out, "Stop, don't talk, Holy Moses! I see your third eye looking right at me!" His head made a jolt. With a shocked reaction in his normal eyes, he said nothing. I had frequently heard there was such a thing as a third eye, but, until that moment, I had never really believed it!

We left the building without further conversation. While driving in his car, he invited me to dinner. He said it was too late for a meal in a restaurant and he was afraid I wouldn't find a place to have some food before I went to sleep. He told me he had a friend who had a hotel and we could have room service in one of the rooms. When I had finished my meal, I thanked him, and asked to be taken to my hotel. I think he had other plans. It wasn't until the next morning, as I dizzily got up early to catch my plane that I realized I had been drugged the night before.

When I arrived at the airport in Cairo, my husband was waiting to meet my plane. The place was in an uproar because one of the American couples who had come for the educational conference had opened their suitcase for inspection and their cat had jumped out and run away. Unknowingly, their cat had somehow got into their luggage. They were very upset, and were calling and looking for their cat. All of the other Americans tried to help them, but no one ever found it. The Egyptian inspectors couldn't figure out why people were making such a fuss over an animal.

We had the use of a friend's apartment for the conference. From the balcony, at night you could see the lights on the pyramids. I sat outside to meditate. The air was balmy and the breeze comforting. Instantly I went into a very deep space and, while there, saw an image of a beautiful blue bird rise up before me. It was an intense sensation. I readily knew that it had special significance. During breakfast, I told my husband that my meditation the night before was so strange and that, because of it, I thought someone very near to me in America had died.

I wondered if it could have been my mother. He laughed and said, "Just some more of your insane ideas."

The next morning, I went to the King Tut Museum. I hired a guide to take me on a quick tour because I was short of time. After an hour or so, while walking past a large mural, we stopped because I had a question. "What is the significance of that blue bird flying upward?"

He replied, "The Egyptians believed that when you die, the blue bird carries your soul out of your body."

I said, "I saw that bird last night in my meditation."

He exclaimed, "Then you have a white heart!"

I stood still in my tracks and called out, "What does that mean?"

He answered, "Some people have black hearts, but yours is white." I thanked him and told him that the tour was over. I went to a café to think while having coffee.

My mind immediately recalled the Inca initiation. The man who performed the service wore an Egyptian robe. My Inca name, WHUAKA YURAC ZONKO, meant the cleansing of the white heart! Did these two experiences have anything to do with each other? Were they connected? Did this mean that my heart had been cleansed?

When I got home, I didn't tell my husband about what had happened. We called to the United States and my mother, fortunately, was alive and well. I felt like I had given him another reason to ridicule me.

Lesson Ten – The Beast

We returned to the United States and my abnormal life continued. The children were away at school and my husband was off for long periods of time living his own private life. We had tried a trial separation before we went to live in Africa and, for the sake of the children, hoped for a new reuniting of the marriage. Now we saw that the reuniting wasn't happening, but we still hung on to each other. I needed someone to confide in, so I would tell him about the crazy things that were happening to me. Things like seeing the third eye and the bluebird. He would tell me that if I didn't stop this crazy behavior, I would become insane. I was alone and didn't know how to react to my inner life.

In New Brunswick, where we were living, I had a friend who was the wife of my husband's best friend. When I was out of town, she, her husband, and my husband would drink and party together. One day when she and I (after a few drinks), were chatting, she asked me about a woman who lived in Texas. She gave me the person's name and said my husband had told her this lady was his woman in the port of Galveston. My friend went on to say that he had said he had a woman at each port or station wherever he did his overseas work. When I heard the name of the woman from Texas, I knew that she was the wife of a man who worked so hard to get EOA off the ground. He worked long hours in the Galveston/Houston area, and he and his wife lived on a very low salary. We all worked toward a hope in the future when we would get enough students for the program to make money.

The thought of my husband taking advantage of a man who had sacrificed so much, and had honestly tried to help us, sickened me. I couldn't believe he was the same person whom I had married. That night when we got into bed, I told him what our friend had said. His reaction was, "They are separating and I am saving the marriage." I asked him if this man knew that he was sleeping with his wife. He answered, "No." I was quiet for some time, then I informed my husband that I no longer was his woman at the port of New Brunswick (there is no port in New Brunswick), and that I no longer wanted a sexual relationship with him. He rolled over and went to sleep.

While lying in bed thinking about how easily he had fallen asleep, I began to feel some eyes looking at me. I raised myself up and looked in the direction that I felt the force coming from. It was out of the upstairs window. Too frightened to react, I became aware of a huge head with two very large eyes. It had a fierce gaze and was pouring an angry stare directly at my face. Intuitively, there was no doubt that this was the beast that ruled sexuality. He had smooth looking skin, rounded roly-poly cheeks, and a cunning, curled mouth smile. There were no words uttered, but I felt the sensation of, "I'll get you, little honey. There is no contest between your power and mine. I am about to devour you!" I couldn't see his body, but I felt that he must have been sitting cross-legged on the ground. He felt enormous and clever, certainly no match for me. I think in India he would be called an asuric (negative) being. I guess we call it a demon.

I crawled out of bed and facing him, sat in a big soft armchair so my back would be covered. I thought facing him would put me in a position of more control in case he came after me. I fully realized that I should go to the kitchen and get some plastic to wrap around my heart and chest so his vibrations couldn't enter me. I had learned that from Alex. I usually slipped a plastic garment bag with the head and arms cut out over my body, but now I had no time for either of these things. With a thick blanket covering my front, and realizing it really wasn't protecting me, I stayed awake until the morning dawned because I thought if I went to sleep, he would overtake my consciousness. As I sat there, I wondered if my husband was right, "Was I going mad?" There were so many strange events constantly happening in my life. Why?

We left New Brunswick. My husband went back on the road and I moved to Michigan to work the migrant program. Everything was in a mess. All of our savings had been used for EOA. I had a broken down, older car, but at least I had work that I loved and I could live with my mother.

Jim Goure, the guru from North Carolina, frequently came to Grand Rapids. He happened to be there for a weekend retreat soon after I arrived. We had a private session, and I told him about the beast. He said "SO, YOU HAVE SEEN THE BEAST!"

His words saved me. I wasn't crazy. There really is such a thing as a beast! I could have hugged and hugged and hugged Jim Goure. "Thank God I wasn't going mad!"

I also told Jim about the time that I had the scar from shingles. I explained the capital letter M on my chest. When I had completed the story, I said, "I could have taken a picture of it, but I didn't because I felt if people didn't believe me, so what! Taking a picture is to satisfy ego."

Jim jumped up from his chair. His actions were like, "Glory, Glory! Hallelujah!" He yelled, "I love you, woman, I love you!"

Two weeks later in a dream, and later in a follow-up discussion about the dream with a friend who was a psychoanalyst, I realized that my marriage had truly ended. The dream was powerful, with great clarity. I was driving my Fiat, my favorite little car, on a street next to the entrance of Central Park in New York City. I came to a stoplight and was waiting for the light to change. It was pouring rain. Another car pulled up next to mine. Suddenly, a man jumped out of his car, came over to my car, and tore the wipers off my windshield. He came up to the closed window by the driver's seat. With dramatic intent, he placed both hands on his hips, and with a nasty glare, stuck his face looking directly into my face. He said, "There," meaning, "Take that!"

I yelled, "You bastard!" With my windshield wipers in his hands, he got back into his car and, when the light changed, he drove away. I sat helpless in the pouring rain. Everything was a blur.

The psychoanalyst talked with me again and within minutes I clearly understood the meaning of the dream. He cleverly clarified the situation as he asked me some pertinent questions. He said, "A car usually means your road of life. You were driving your car down your road of life and then what happened?"

I answered, "I stopped and a man took my windshield wipers."

He said, "What do wipers do?"

I said, "They clear your vision." I then realized that I couldn't drive down my road of life because someone didn't want me to see where I was going. Without vision, I wouldn't accomplish my goal!

My friend asked, "Who was the man?" As he spoke, I remembered the round face in the dream. I had an Aha! moment! Without hesitation, I called out, "It was my husband!"

He said, "Is there anything else to say? You have answered your own questions."

Lesson Eleven – Love is the Answer

When I was teaching the migrant program, I was very satisfied with my work. I adored the children and the program was a challenge. My life, however, on the outside was a bust. There were no Sri Aurobindo groups in the area; however, I found a place (the Vedanta Retreat Center), where they would allow me to follow my own guru and still be a part of their groups. I spent Sundays there with friends. After the potluck meal, I would drive home along the road that followed the Lake Michigan shoreline. During the summer months, I always stopped at a hot dog stand, bought coffee, and sat on a bench near the water reading a book.

There were many benches. I went to one that was isolated from the rest. A somewhat younger man had the same idea. He always sat on the other end of the bench. Week after week, to be polite, we would nod to greet each other every time one of us sat down. He once noticed the cover of the book I was reading and we got into a long discussion. I finished the book and gave it to him to take home to read. The following week, we got into an exciting conversation. We began to look forward to our weekly meetings. Sometime later, our conversations extended to going out for evening meals. Eventually, it took us into the bedroom.

Each time I would get involved with a man, I would always ask the Mother, "Is this what You want?" Of course, She didn't directly answer me. I had to figure that out for myself. I took a huge picture of Her and put it in the bedroom. I said to Her, "Now You are in the center of the matter, so please help me figure out what You want." In the beginning of this relationship, because of his age, I had no long-term plan with this man. Age didn't seem to bother him.

Our minds clicked. He was very intelligent and was amazed at my ability to readily comprehend concepts. He kept referring to the speed of my brain. In spite of his intelligence, he needed time to think. Each week he would come back with conclusions that he had come to because of our previous conversations. New-age topics fascinated us and no far-out idea would be too exaggerated to consider. The relationship was exciting and fun. To this day, although we have not seen each other for years, I miss him. When I encounter a new idea, I automatically think of him and how much fun we would have figuring it out. Now I frequently let those ideas go, because I don't have him (or anyone else), to help energize the search for conclusions.

The fly in the ointment came when I met a close friend of his. He took me aside and said, "I want to warn you to be on guard because my friend can be an unscrupulous opportunist." I had somewhat come to that conclusion and was beginning to realize that this relationship was an assignment (that is the way I interpret my work, for Her, as assignments), from the Mother. I greatly admired his friend for trying to protect me. My relationship with this man continued off and on for seven years. It was interrupted months at a time because I would go to Florida while the migrant children went back to Texas.

My schedule with my students began on March 1st, when their parents arrived to plant the new seedlings at the tree nursery. They worked until October 31st. My teaching schedule was continuous, spring, summer and fall. In October, they went to Texas and I went to Florida. Usually I would not see my friend for four months. Once in a while, he would drive to Florida with me, stay a few months, and then fly back to Michigan.

Frequently, from my point of view, the relationship with the younger man was a bit stormy. I kept asking the Mother if this really was what She had in mind. While doing an assignment, I completely rode on my gut feeling as to what I thought was needed. You are never sure that you have interpreted Her needs correctly. I kept guessing and hoping I was doing what She wanted. The repeated message from Her to me was, "Turn the other cheek. No matter what this man does, no matter how outrageous his behavior becomes, turn the other cheek. Give him opportunities to make the right choices and when he doesn't, present him with a chance to make the same mistake over and over again." It was a difficult relationship.

One year when I returned from Florida, I went to his place to see him. He was sitting under a tree reading. At first glance, I wondered what had happened to him because he didn't look the same. He had a roly-poly belly. I found myself thinking, "Whoa, he looks heavy!" As he turned his face and smiled, I noticed something eerie about the look in his eyes (it still gives me a chill). Something was different, but I couldn't put my finger on what the difference was. The next time I saw him, I realized that what I had seen in him was the appearance of the beast. I shuddered and went home.

That night I had another of those dreams that is beyond a dream. A swarm of little beasts were attacking me. They came from every direction and each had a penis in his hand. Each beast was trying to stuff my eyes, nose, ears, and mouth with his penis. I was being bombarded. Then my friend, this same male friend, came to my rescue. In the dream, he put his arms around me, with his back to them, to protect me. He said to the swarm of little beasts, "Not her." The swarm immediately disappeared. They reacted as if someone high in command had just spoken.

I got out of bed and went to the bathroom. As I was washing my hands I looked in the mirror. Looking back at me were the eyes of Sri Aurobindo. There was a feeling of great joy in His expression. Stunned, I walked into the living room and went into a song and dance like I have never done before. I was stomping and clapping and yelling from the inside out. I was full of glee. Like a crazed woman, I danced in circles around and around. I kept watching my own legs doing a high stepping stomp. As rapidly as I began this behavior, I stopped it. I thought, "This is not me, I don't even know why I'm so happy." That was the first moment that I recognized how much the Mother was using me. I was sobered by the whole incident. Not that I cared, I was just surprised by my own behavior.

I asked myself, "What happened? Why are Sri Aurobindo and the Mother spontaneously jubilant? What occurrence has stimulated such behavior on Their part?" Thinking back, I realized that, because of love, the beast was brought to his knees. Love is the answer! The next time I saw my friend, he said, "I don't know what happened, but something inside of me has changed." I said nothing. Whatever happened to his inner self wasn't a complete transformation, because soon he was up to his old, unscrupulous behavior again. By the reaction of the two gurus, I am led to believe that a breakdown of the beast has begun and that I had stepped into the mire of life and brought some light.

Lesson Twelve – I Woke Up!

After the incident I just related, when I was doing some kind of a wild dance of uninhibited joy, I woke up. From that time on, I realized how much the Mother really was using me. I didn't know it then, but She was about to show me just how much She was directing the show. Her next, even stranger, happening occurred for my benefit.

Each time I returned to Florida, I would try to see Jim Goure at United Research in Black Mountain, North Carolina. I would stop on the way up and on the way back. There was always hope that he might be giving some interesting lectures or a conference. One lucky weekend, he was having three days of talks. He asked me to stay, but I told him I was on my way back to work and didn't have extra money. He invited me to attend the conference and sleep at his house. His place was very large, with many bedrooms. He had eight children, and most of them hadn't been around for some time because they were either at a university or were married.

A part of the house was a remodeled lodge. My room was in that section of the house. When I went to bed, the room was silent for a while and then I heard the sound of mice running helter-skelter on the floor above me. First of all, I wasn't sure they were mice because they made too much noise. My daughter has two cats and I frequently hear the sound of their feet at night. I now realize that what I heard was the sound of a cat running on the floor above me and not mice or rats. At that time, I only hoped they weren't rats. I thought, "Get a hold on your-self, Jim wouldn't have a place that has rats!"

I wasn't about to turn on the light and check out the situation. A short time later, I heard a cat meow. The sound was so loud I knew it wasn't a kitten. It meowed again nearer to my bed. At first, I was in shock, really somewhat afraid. I said, "Don't be ridiculous, a cat isn't going to hurt you," (I'm not a cat person). I reached my arm out from under the blanket to the side of my bed and called, "Here kitty, kitty, here kitty, kitty." It surely wasn't a kitty, but what else could I say, "here cat, here cat?" I was half expecting to feel a furry head under my extended hand, nothing happened. I breathed a sigh of relief, pulled the blankets up to my neck, covered my face with a sheet, and said, "I'll deal with this in the morning."

At breakfast, Jim and I were alone, as his wife had gone shopping. I asked him if there was a cat in the house. He looked at me in a strange way and said, "Why do you ask?" I told him the story of the night before when a cat was meowing in my room. He looked at me and with great force in his voice said, "There have been over three thousand people who have come to this house. Some of them accomplished gurus, and none of them has been able to do what you did last night (materialize a cat). Woman, when are you going to wake up and start to do the work you have come to do?" He finished his coffee and left the room.

I sat there in a daze, shaking my head in disbelief. In his eyes, I had materialized a cat! I shook and shook my head in absolute wonderment. I was too stunned to say, "It must have been the Mother." I later remembered that She was a student of the occult and could do whatever She wanted to do. I thought, "Is this so strange? After all, Jesus could change water into wine!"

Jim didn't say anything when I came to his morning lecture. He just looked at me and shook his head. He was always after me to give up my teaching career and join a group of spiritually-minded people. That is why he paid my conference fee. Jim felt the time for gurus as teachers was over. In his lectures, he informed everyone that each of us was a co-creator and we could do what gurus do.

I thought he really didn't understand how completely I was tied up with the Mother, and that I was doing spiritual work with and for Her. He saw Her as just another guru from India. To leave a teaching career never entered the equation because I needed the security of a paycheck. I had two children who needed to go to college. After three days, I left the conference, and while driving home, I kept thinking, "She materialized a cat! If it wasn't a cat, which I didn't see, I was sure that twice I heard a loud meow." I smiled all the way home.

The Mother was ready to show me one more of Her abilities. I was visiting my friend, Geri, in Massachusetts. Her daughter owned a very upscale boutique and Geri wanted me to see it and meet her daughter. We dressed in our better clothes because we didn't want to embarrass anyone in case there were some fancy costumers in the shop. Three very stylish young ladies greeted us as we stepped into the store. One of them was her daughter and the other two worked for her. My friend also worked for her daughter, so she intimately knew all three of these young ladies.

Geri enthusiastically introduced me to each person. After a few moments of small talk, it was time for them to get back to work. Geri and one of the young ladies went into the back room. I was walking from one display to another, touching the fabrics, and checking out the styles of the garments. Each piece of merchandise expressed the outstanding ability of the owner to select exquisite fabrics and designs.

Before I became an art teacher, I had attended the Fashion Academy in New York City. As I looked at these clothes, my mind wandered back to those years, and I wondered how extremely different my life would have been as a fashion illustrator. My daydreaming suddenly was interrupted. Sobbing sounds were coming from the back room, and Geri was saying, "Tell Shirley, she will understand."

I listened and thought, "What are they talking about? What will I understand?"

Geri repeated, "Tell her!" Soon a very attractive, dark haired, sobbing, young woman approached me at a counter in the middle of the room. She was crying so hard I couldn't understand one word she tried to say. We held hands.

She took some time to calm herself down and then tried to speak, instead she burst into tears. After a few more attempts, she finally took control of herself and said, "A few weeks ago, on Christmas Eve, when I went to a Catholic Church service, there were statues of Jesus and the twelve apostles in the entryway. They were dressed in long-hooded robes. Each head was bent in prayer. As I came in, one of them raised his head and looked into my eyes. She started to cry. Between blurts of sobs, she said, "Those were your eyes." Now we both needed to calm down. After some time, who knows how long, I collected my thoughts and asked which apostle had raised his head? She answered, "Jesus," and began to sob again. I can't tell you what I did next. This was the shock of shocks! As we started to leave, she said, "My ex-husband once had those eyes too!" Perplexed? You can be sure I was!

One of the difficult problems during a development of spirituality is the knowledge that there are entities on another dimension that can imitate anyone and do anything they want to do. Above all, what they do not want is for you to succeed in finding the White Light. They are masters in their games of deception. Their desire is to lead you down the wrong path. They are extremely clever and seem very authentic. One must always be on guard to decipher darkness from light.

This spiritual work is a constant vigilance and the situation in front of me demanded a close examination of what was occurring. How could I have the same look in my eyes as her husband had in his eyes? She was divorcing him. Was this a dark force playing a game with me? I'm not afraid to face a dark force because the Mother is always at my side. At times during this lifetime, I have been at the depth of despair, at the gates of hell, and at other times fused with the White Light. The deeper you dare to step into darkness, the higher you go into the light. One balances out the other. My hope is that with faith in my inner guidance and the grace of Sri Aurobindo and the Mother (They are One), I will detect the right path to follow. My question for the moment was, "Is this a dark or light force?" By putting no more energy into the incident, it soon passed.

Lesson Thirteen – Shock!

September of 1992 I retired. Now I could go to the Ashram and stay until March 1st, when it gets too hot for me to live in southern India. There are two choices to contemplate when you arrive. You can choose the Ashram, which is made up of around one thousand two hundred devotees (mostly from India), or you can live ten kilometers from there in Auroville, which has almost as many people as the Ashram has. Most of the people in Auroville were European or Indian. Now they come from the all corners of the world.

Both groups are followers of Sri Aurobindo and the Mother, but the way they live is quite distinct. In the beginning, the Mother developed the Ashram for the followers of Sri Aurobindo. At first, it was only for devotees, but, in time, it included their families. That was the reason for developing the Sri Aurobindo International Center of Education.

The Mother had a large following in Paris. When She decided there should be one place on earth where people could follow their hearts without the need to be concerned with money and greed, She developed Auroville (the city of Dawn). Many from Her group in Paris sold all of their possessions and brought the money to the Mother. She developed a community with the aim of working on human unity.

AUROVILLE-MATRIMANDIR

*"There should be somewhere on the earth a place
which no nation could claim as its own, where
all human beings of goodwill who have a sincere
aspiration could live freely as citizens of the world and
obey one single authority, that of the supreme.*

The MOTHER

In 1972, when my son and I first arrived in Pondicherry, many of the Western people who lived there were of the Ashram. Those were the people we got to know and most of them later became Aurovillians. When you arrived, you went to the Ashram work office to see how you could help. They would tell you where you should go to do community service. Over the years, I have worked in the eye clinic, education department, and in the kitchen drying dishes of stainless steel. To this day, many Aurovillians go to the Ashram because the meditation area (Samadhi) of Sri Aurobindo and The Mother is there. Few Ashramites visit Auroville. That is beginning to change because of the Matrimandir (picture), an amazing building which is the temple of the Mother at the heart of Auroville.

This time I decided to go to Auroville. I figured I would give service as an art teacher in the Auroville School. A taxi took me to the Center Guest House. Not only did I teach art for a month, I also took over a second grade classroom because the teacher's mother was ill and she had to go back to the Netherlands. Because I was giving service to the community, I could lodge at the Guest House for the entire time I was in India. I wasn't an Aurovillian, so I had to pay for my room, but usually you can only live in a guest house for a limited amount of time. Every Saturday, the Auroville bus took people to the Ashram in the city of Pondicherry. I would always take the Auroville bus and share with others the price of the six mile taxi ride to get home.

On this trip to India, I hoped to answer the riddle of why, twenty years ago, my name was all in red capitals on the board for collecting letters from the Mother. Shivani had lived there for some time and she had never seen it before. I had only been there a few months, but I knew a few people quite well and I couldn't figure out why no one had said anything about it. Nolinida, when he handed me the letter from out of a large red folder, had said nothing. Later, when I returned and said, "I don't understand," he had folded his hands, made two slight bows, and said, "You will, you will." My question was, "When?" Nolinida had left his body and I had no idea whom I should ask. I knew it was only a matter of time because I was determined to find out what this mystery was all about.

In the Ashram bookstores I would frequently see displays of new books by M.P. Pandit. Sometimes his picture was on the back of the book, so I knew what he looked like. I had seen his picture many times before, so I knew he must be someone important. As you went to the meditation room of the Mother, you had to pass an area where you could buy only his books. This time, when I passed that place, he was sitting on a chair just inside of the shop. I stepped up my courage and approached him. He responded with a soft, inviting smile. I timidly said, "Twenty years ago at this Ashram I had an experience that has never been explained. I wonder if I tell you about it, could you tell me what it means?"

He smiled, handed me a small piece of paper with his address on it, and said, "Come to my house tomorrow at three o'clock."

"I said, "Thank you," and walked away.

The next afternoon, I knocked at his door and a woman let me in. M.P. Pandit was seated in a chair waiting for me. We talked for some time. I showed him the small packet with the gold framed, smiling picture of the Mother. He examined it carefully and opened it to see the date written with a red pen in the hand of the Mother. With sincere reverence, he took it in his hands and touched it to his forehead. We talked awhile and then discussed the topic I had come for. I asked him if he could tell me why the letters of my name were written in the color red and why the letters were capitals."What did that mean?"

He said, "It means the Divine has descended."

I looked at him as if he were ridiculous. I said, "WHAT?"

He repeated, "The Divine has descended!"

We sat there, wordless for a moment, looking into each other's eyes. I must have had a look of shock on my face, because that's how I felt. When I regained my composure, I said, "What should I do about this?"

He was silent. He had an expressionless look on his face, as if to say, "Who knows, or nothing!" I stood up and so did he. I thanked him for his time and left the house. I was too stunned to meditate. I got a taxi and went back to the guest house.

A few weeks later, having said nothing to anyone, I flew to the United States. I had come to India to celebrate my retirement, Auroville's 25th birthday, and now something else. When I returned, seven years later, M.P. Pandit had left his body. In fact, everyone who could have validated my stories had left: Norman Dowsett, Nolinida, M.P. Pandit, Jim Goure, and Alex.

Lesson Fourteen – Chance Meeting

At this point, I want to take you back to the time when I was in India with my son. We were about to leave the Ashram because he decided he didn't want to stay in school at =1 (I haven't related to you an incident that happened the day before we left). I didn't know how to deal with it earlier in this book and I'm not at ease with it now. I sometimes wonder if I should deal with it at all, but since it is a part of my history with the Mother, and that's the purpose of this book, I place this experience on the table to be examined. My hope is that, by now, you have more of a feeling of who I am, and where I'm coming from, so what I have to say may be more believable. I feel the need to explain this (if it is explainable), before I can go on with my story.

As somewhat of a background, you should know that, because I was in India, I went to an Ayurvedic doctor. He was a member of the Ashram. I had no understanding of Ayurvedic medicine, but I thought I should take advantage of the fact that I had an opportunity to see an authentic practitioner. I really wasn't ill; I just wanted to have my curiosity satisfied. When we sat down across from each other, he placed my hand and wrist in his hands. He wanted to feel my vibration. After some time, he said, "I can't help you because the Mother's grace is upon you." Now, I should have been very pleased with such wonderful news, but if you can recall, at that time, I still didn't have an idea of who this lady was.

The next day, a few hours before we were ready to take a taxi to Madras, I was walking on a sidewalk along a large Ashram building. I came to the corner and coming from the other side of the building, so we would meet each other at the corner, I ran into Norman Dowsett. He was the director of the Ashram Education Department. I had worked for him and, along with his secretary, had gone to many of his lectures. He is the same man who told me that I should write a note to the Mother when I had that feeling of a hole in my back. As we almost collided, he was startled and said, "I was just told that the next woman I meet is going to be the next Mother and that is you!" His statement was expressed as a matter of fact. He continued on his way as if nothing had happened. I stood there watching him leave. Red letters, the hole in my back, and now this!

My reaction was, "Is he nuts or what? Norman, why would you say such a thing? I know you; we have worked together for two months. What is this all about? In the first place, there will never be another Mother and, in the second place, who would want the responsibility of coming after a force like that?" I thought, "My God! This place is becoming more and more extreme, everyday there is something new to deal with! Leaving this city can't come soon enough. I must get my son out of here!" I was so happy that my daughter hadn't come with us.

I have never had a chance to talk to Norman about this moment because years later when I returned for a visit, he had passed away. On this return visit, I again went to see the Ayurvedic doctor. He expressed his surprise at the complete surrender he found in my devotion to the Mother. He was speechless with his emotion.

Now, forty-two years have passed since Sri Aurobindo came to me, and it is possible to put this information in some kind of context. I have become aware of the fact that there are many men and women who have surrendered to the Mother in order to do Her work. I feel that if we all stood up, there would be a surprising number of Aurovillians and Ashramites who have an assignment given to them by Her.

The last time I visited the Ashram, I saw an example of this. I was privileged to have had a meditation with a woman who is completely devoted to the Mother. During that meditation, at the Samadhi of Sri Aurobindo, I saw the Mother as She had been when I gave Her the flowers. She was sitting in the place of this woman. It was not a solid body. Rather, it was an ethereal, filmy substance. The Mother is here, and some of us have surrendered to Her so She can direct us to help further Her mission for this planet.

I want to clarify the difference between surrendering my body for the use of the Mother to do Her work and that of a Walk-In. A Walk-in is a person who has come from another dimension and walked into the body of a person on the planet earth. In the case of a Walk-In, the original person who gave up their body for someone else to walk into is no longer there. The person who walks in wants a shortcut into life. They do not want to go through birth, childhood, or adolescence.

Walk-Ins are spiritually guided and have come to serve humanity. I once met and told a Walk-In (she had written a book about her life as a Walk-In), of my situation with the Mother. I explained that it felt like two people, the Mother and me, living inside of one body. She replied, "I don't see it that way, I see it as you have been like Her shadow." I have met three people, one very well-known and from good authority, two others, who consider themselves Walk-ins. One is the director of a Mystery School and the Mother used her to teach me an important step in my personal growth and spiritual development. The experience that I needed to have done to me could not have been done by just anyone and it had to have had a personal (in the physical) touch. The fact that the Mother chose her to do this special spiritual work, here on this planet, helped me verify the value of Walk-Ins.

My life since I was forty-two years old has been one of assignments for the Mother. The problem is that during the process you don't know that it's an assignment and frequently you don't realize that you are being tested. You have to pass the smaller tests in order to qualify for more difficult assignments. The only inkling you have that you are being tested is by your gut feelings. Either you go with them or you don't. There are no lesson plans. It's all up to you and how you view and react to the situation in front of you. It may sound like the Mother is taking advantage of me. That is not the case. From the first time I was in Her presence, somehow I intuitively understood the importance of Her mission (to transform humanity), and knew what I should do with my life. Auroville and the Ashram are full of people like me, who serve the Mother.

Lesson Fifteen – An Aurovillian

I was determined to discover if anyone besides M.P. Pandit knew the meaning of the red letters. I needed someone else to verify what he had told me at his house that afternoon in India. I couldn't imagine that someone, out of more than a thousand people at the Ashram, had not noticed those red letters on the bulletin board. Shivani had rushed over to my house to inform me. She was just a teenager and she knew that something significantly different had occurred. Someone else must have had some kind of reaction, but who could it be? That was my charge, to locate some other person who had seen the bulletin board and knew the answer. When I told a friend how dumbfounded I was that no one had said anything to me about it, she responded, "Maybe they thought you knew."

One of the original devotees of Sri Aurobindo was still living. He was over ninety-years old and I thought he was my best chance for a straight answer. I got excited when I was allowed to speak to him for a short time. It turned out to be a very short time because he could not answer my question. I encountered many older Ashramites who would have been in the Ashram in 1972, when this happened, but none of them had the slightest idea as to what the meaning of the red letters could be. One man's remark was, "Maybe She only had a red pen." I knew that wasn't the answer because when Nolinida gave me my letter from the Mother, it was in a large red folder. I knew the answer to the meaning of the color red was what I was looking for.

The Center Guest House in Auroville was near an open-air lecture area. I heard there was going to be a speech at that place on the following Sunday afternoon. A man who wrote some very important books about the life of the Mother would deliver the lecture, and there would be a question and answer period when he finished. The speaker had done an extensive study of every aspect of Her amazing life, so I thought he might have some information that would help me. When the lecture was over, we made arrangements to meet at the Auroville café. After hearing my story, he had no comments.

The following Sunday there was another exciting program at the same location. This time the speakers would be people who had actually had a one-on-one experience with the Mother. I went early to speak to the program organizer. When we sat down, I explained how I had met the Mother and was in Auroville for a short visit and might not be back for years. I informed her I would be happy to relate my story if she needed another speaker. When it was my turn to speak, I told the audience I was like a butterfly that flew in and out of India to come to the Ashram and Auroville as frequently as possible. I informed them that this was my sixth trip and I was happy to be there.

The story of Sri Aurobindo coming to me in Barcelona and, four years later, the good fortune of meeting the Mother, excited everyone. The crowd reacted with pleasure when I told them of the mistake of giving the Mother the flower "Surrender," instead of the flower "Psychological Perfection." I spoke for twenty minutes and when I finished, people from the audience came up and suggested I write a book.

As we were beginning to leave the gathering, I asked to speak again to the program director, who was a woman from India. Over the past years, I had seen her many times and observed that she was an important figure in Auroville. We sat down for just a short time because she had another appointment. When I showed her the tiny packet of dried flowers with the thin, gold framed picture of the Mother, she opened it like a book and saw inside the date, in red, in the Mother's handwriting. With extremely delicate care, this lady examined the packet. A tender expression came into her eyes and in a soft, loving voice she said, "The Mother has given you a special gift." I thanked her for sharing her time with me. We got up and went our separate ways. The next day, I was leaving India. I left wishing I could spend more time with this woman to see if she had any additional information for me. My only hope was that she would still be there in the future when I returned.

I was sitting on the airplane, wondering if I would ever live at the Ashram or in Auroville. Each time I would go to India to visit, I hoped to see some signs from the Mother that it was time for me to stay. I didn't care what place it would be. Living under Her influence is so calming and helpful. I wanted to be near Her. Each time the answer was the same, "Not yet." I felt my work for Her was in America and She would let me know when it was completed.

As many times as I had been to Auroville, had worked there, and mixed with people I had known before, I never seemed to be other than a stranger. I guessed it was because I had always lived in a guest house and never ate in the Auroville dining room. It felt as though too much time had passed between visits, so I never got to know anyone really well.

In an unexpected way, my lack of a close contact with an Aurovillian changed, and it happened in America. I am writing this book while living, during the winter months, in Florida. I write and then send my work to my cousin, Barbara, in California. I mail copies of pages that I have completed to her. She edits and types them, burns a disk, and sends the printed pages back to me. Each time I send more pages, I make copies at the 7-Eleven Store near my apartment. When I was ready to send her the mail, I felt it was time to send a picture of Sri Aurobindo, so she would understand more about the mysterious man I was constantly writing about. I took a book that had His picture on the cover and made a copy. When I finished, I put the book face up on the seat in the car and went across the street to the post office to mail her the package.

I had spent about twenty minutes running back and forth to the copy machine. Each time I returned to the car, I had noticed the same woman standing in the shade in front of the library, which was next to the post office. It was too hot to be just standing outside, so I suspected this woman was waiting for someone to pick her up. The library closed early that day and I thought she hadn't known that. Returning from the post office, I was on her side of the street and walking toward her.

I had specifically stayed on that side so I could ask her if she needed a ride home. Before I could say anything, she said, "I like your dress."

A bit startled, I answered, "Thank you, it was made in India."

Her response was, "I know."

I proceeded to inquire about her situation. Did she need a ride? She explained that she was visiting her mother who lived at a retirement complex and someone from there was going to pick her up for a ride home in half an hour. The address of her mother's place was only five miles away, so I said, "Jump in the car. We can get there before the driver leaves."

She hesitated and asked, "Are you sure you want to do this?"

I replied, "Yes, I'm retired, time doesn't mean anything to me. Your mother doesn't live far from here."

As she got into the car, she saw the book. With a surprised sound in her voice, she said, "Oh, Sri Aurobindo!"

I reacted with utter dismay. "Do you know about Sri Aurobindo?"

She laughed and said, "I live in Auroville."

Shocked, I gasped while reeling my head in her direction. "You live in Auroville. I go to Auroville! I've been there six times!" We both laughed.

She said, "You look like an Aurovillian."

I said, "This dress was made there."

We laughed again as she grinned and said, "I know."

As we spoke, we realized we knew many of the same people. She asked why I wasn't living in Auroville. I told her there wasn't any senior housing, to which she responded, "There is now, they are in the process of building the apartments as we speak." She went on to explain that someone I knew was developing a new community called Creativity.

We arrived at the retirement apartments and I went in to meet her mother. That evening, Bhavana, my new Aurovillian friend, was giving a presentation with a video about Auroville. I stayed for the meeting, and the next day we had a short time to chat. I told her I was writing a book. She suggested I put one of my flower paintings on the front page. The next day, she saw the paintings and still thought I should put one in the book. Bhavana stayed in America on the west coast for many months before returning to India, so we had time for telephone conversations. What amazes me about our chance meeting (chance???) is the fact that I had the book with the picture of Sri Aurobindo in my car for one day. That was the day I met her. Perhaps the telling of this episode will help you realize just how much the Mother directs my life. As soon as I found out that Auroville had senior housing, I called to see if there were any available units. The answer was positive and I eagerly anticipated going to India to look at what was still unoccupied. Before I bought the ticket, I found out that I had cancer. My house in Michigan had just sold and while packing a large amount of heavy books to give to the monastery, a soft lump developed on the left side of my neck. I had been so busy for so many days that I hadn't noticed it begin to grow. I would shower before I went to bed, the next morning dress with blouses that covered my neck, and then get on with my day. I didn't wear makeup, so there wasn't a reason to look into the mirror. In my eyes, a lump had suddenly appeared.

It took five visits to different doctors, six CAT scans, and a biopsy before I knew that what I was dealing with was Level-1, non-aggressive, Non-Hodgkin's Lymphoma, which meant that, hopefully, my life wouldn't change, except for visits every three months to a specialist to watch that the few lymph nodes didn't enlarge. No treatments. I had a bone marrow test which indicated my body was not developing cancer cells. However, because of the appointments, I would have to stay, off and on, in America for the next two years. That was news I did not want to hear.

During that period, I didn't know what type of cancer I had and because I thought it happened almost overnight; I had a real scare. An artist friend of mine had died in three months after she had been diagnosed with cancer of the pancreas. I had handled and worked with the same artist's materials that she had handled, so I thought my days were numbered. I sat up nights writing this book and good-bye notes.

I could view this incident as a way for the Mother to keep me in America, or a way to hurry me with the writing of the book. One never knows what the reason might be. To me, there was a reason. This episode took six months out of my life. My inner feelings told me that the Mother's message still was, "Not yet."

Lesson Sixteen – The Color Red

The meeting with Bhavana in front of the library on that hot sunny day resulted in further implications. As I mentioned before, we had talked on the phone on a few different occasions during her stay in America and, because her brother lived near Boston and my daughter lived in the next state, we thought we would have a chance to meet again before she returned to India. That didn't happen because she stayed at the Sri Aurobindo Ashram in Lodi, California, for longer than expected. When she left, she sent me a packet of information about Auroville centers in the United States.

One particular center caught my attention because five years earlier friends from Chicago had mentioned that there was going to be an Auroville elementary school in San Francisco. That school had now become the Center for Integral Education in San Diego. This year they were beginning grades one and two. I had always wanted to volunteer and those grades were where I had done most of my teaching. I had developed innovative programs and I thought I might be of some help.

I was scheduled to fly to San Francisco for a family wedding on the 19th of February. There are many Aurobindo centers near there. The Ashram where Bhavana stayed is less than two hours away. With a sense of great joy, I remembered that the Mother's birthday was on the 21st of February, so I changed my plans and made arrangements for an extended stay.

I arrived at Lodi when it was getting dark and got a hotel room for one night. Neither the clerk nor the manager had information about the location of the Ashram. When they saw the address, they could only point to some place near, but out of town. I got up at nine o' clock the next morning. I didn't want an earlier rise because I was still on Florida hours and I had a long airplane ride the day before. When I arrived at the center on the Mother's birthday, it was too late. They had a sunrise service and now most of the guests had left to drive home. I introduced myself as the person Bhavana had met in front of the library in Florida. The ten people who were still there had heard the story from her, so I was welcomed with open arms. The meditation room was full of roses and mixed flowers. It looked like everyone who came had brought some. The smell in the room was more than pleasant. Mostly it expressed the love that everyone had for the Mother. The conversation during the evening meal evolved into an update on the progress of the school in San Diego.

When I returned to Florida, I called the school and had a lengthy conversation with the person in charge. We discussed the possibility of a visit. I explained my meeting with Bhavana and suggested he call her if he wanted more information about me. We agreed that, one week before school started in the fall, I would come to visit the school and see if I could be of service to him or his teachers. He called back a few days later to say some parents of a child in the school had offered a place for me to stay. They had an extra guest room with a full bath. He asked if I had read *A New Education for a New Consciousness, or Psychic Education*. I said that I hadn't, but assured him that I would order and read the books before I came to his school.

I asked if he was going to attend the upcoming Auroville USA Meeting (AUM) in the state of Washington, and he said that he was. He explained that one full day would be about education. The topic to be studied was Integral Education and Accelerated Evolution (lines of development, the problem of harmony). Then and there, I decided that going to that meeting would be a good way for us to get to know each other and a way to bring me up-to-date with what was happening in education. I registered for the conference.

Every year there was an AUM meeting somewhere in America. It was always in the early part of the summer and I could never attend because of the Migrant Program. This would be my first experience in America with a large group of like-minded people who were followers of Sri Aurobindo and the Mother. I was anxiously waiting for the conference to begin.

The excitement began on the first evening we arrived. Eight strangers were sitting around a large table having coffee. The conversation got around to how we individually had become acquainted with the work of Sri Aurobindo and the Mother. When they heard my story of how he came to me in Barcelona, they were very interested. I mentioned I was writing a book about the experience. As we broke up to leave to hear the next speaker, a young professional man walked up to me and said that a very well-known publishing company had one whole section devoted to the work of Sri Aurobindo and the Mother. He said they had published his book and it wasn't nearly as interesting as my book was going to be (he was being kind and encouraging). He invited me to call him when I finished the book. He would read it because the topic interested him, and also direct the manuscript to the right department at the publishing company. This man was one of the speakers at the conference, so I figured he was dependable. That night in meditation, I thanked the Mother and Bhavana for getting me to this conference.

The following morning, the speaker's statement gave me a jolt. "The Mother had said, "Blessed are those who take a leap into the future." I thought about my dream when I was a student in Mexico. I had stood under the light and stepped into the unknown. That had been a huge leap into the future. When I left Mexico, I came back to America and worked at two jobs to make enough money to go to Spain. I hardly spoke the Spanish language and didn't know anyone in that country, but the Mexican people always spoke endearingly about the mother country, España, and I wanted to see for myself how great that country was.

My mother and a friend drove me to the docks in New York City. She pleaded, with tears in her eyes, "Please don't go; you don't know anyone over there!"

I gave her a goodbye hug and kiss, thanked her for the ride, and said, "Don't worry, I'll be back." I boarded a Greek liner as a third class passenger, and headed for Lisbon. From there, I would catch a train to Seville for the spring fair. Now, sitting at the lecture, I thought, "I was twenty-five years old and I did those things long before I met Sri Aurobindo. Maybe from another dimension He was watching and that is why He came to me, because He saw that I dared to leap into the unknown future."

Another person who had been at the table when I told my story about Barcelona asked if we could sit together for a while so he could question me about my relationship with Sri Aurobindo and the Mother. We never got seated because we were too engrossed in conversation. When I told him that I didn't know how to approach explaining what M.P. Pandit had said about the Divine descending, he hugged me and said "I don't envy you." As he moved to free himself from the hug, he looked into my eyes and, with noticeable changes in the atmosphere and in his voice, he said, "Red is the spark of the supreme essence of the Divine!"

My body quivered. I looked at him with a stare. After a short silence, I said, "What did you say?"

He said, "Red is the color of the physical."

I shook my head and said, "No, that's not what you said!" He shrugged his shoulders as if to say, "I'm sorry but that's all I can recall." I realized that the Mother, through him, had spoken to me. I no longer had to look for someone to verify M.P. Pandit because She had done it. I heard what I was looking for, the meaning of the color red: THE SPARK OF THE SUPREME ESSENCE OF THE DIVINE!

Meeting Bhavana in front of the library was more than chance. There was no doubt in my mind that the Mother had arranged this. From the beginning, I intuitively knew there had to be a reason or reasons for this encounter and now I had to figure out what they were. It was pretty easy to grasp. She informed me about the availability of senior housing, led me to the American Ashram, the Integral Education School, and the conference, where I met the gentleman with information about a book publisher and the answer to the meaning of the color RED!

When a dear friend of mine, who is a monk, read about this chance meeting, his comment was, "This meeting with Bhavana so perfectly illustrates the verse in the Gita (an Indian religious book), which speaks about this guidance by the "subtle pulling of strings" in our lives:

"There lives a Master in the hearts of men,
Who makes their deeds, by subtle pulling of strings,
Dance to what tune he wills.
With all thy soul, trust him, and take him for your support
So, only so, shall you gain, by Grace of Him,
The uttermost repose, the eternal place.

Gita, Chapter 18 verse. 61, Sir Edwin Arnold's translation

Lesson Seventeen – Antahkarana

I was looking forward to the upcoming trip to India, but my physical mind had not finished with its tricks. The cancer scare hadn't been enough. Two weeks before I was ready to leave the country, that mind worked on me again. At four o'clock one morning, while staying at my daughter's house, I left my bed to walk toward the bathroom and became dizzy, veered off to the right, and walked into a wall. I turned around and quickly found my way into the bathroom. I got back into bed and wondered if I should wake my daughter. Was this a stroke? My heart was racing. I held my breath for as long as possible and then let out a strong cough, which usually slowed down my heartbeat. This time it didn't work. I stayed calm and decided to do nothing because that morning was my three month check-up with the cancer doctor.

During the appointment, we talked about my walking into the wall and the dizzy spell. The doctor checked my heart rate, was alarmed, and immediately sent me for an EKG. The heart doctor's report told her that I recently had a slight stroke. I was taken to the emergency room and stayed there the entire night. At eight o'clock the following morning, I was released from the hospital. I was told that I had a strong heart and there was nothing wrong with me. I had the feeling that I had wasted their time. When my children saw the good report, they became less worried about my traveling alone to India.

Upon my arrival at the Center Guest House, I was anxious to find the people from the Ashram and Auroville who, while at the AUM conference, had talked to me about my book. The first person I spoke to suggested I offer the book to Sri Aurobindo on the celebration of the next Darshan. That seemed like an excellent idea, even though I would have to wait four more weeks before I could do so.

During those four weeks, I had changed the place where I was living and had started working as a teacher in one of Auroville's Indian village schools. The headmaster was a friend. On Darshan I would be able to visit the room where Sri Aurobindo had lived, in isolation, for twenty-four years. Devotees went there to honor His memory and to feel His vibration. The teachers and seventy-five children from Isai Ambalam School would attend in the morning, and I was to go with the headmaster a little later in the day. While there, he saw me offer my manuscript. When we left, he asked me if I wanted to share what I had offered. I told him I had written a book. He said he would like to read it.

Two days after he finished reading it, he realized people from a committee he was working with were looking for me. In my book was a story that had been taped during a Sunday afternoon talk by individuals who had a meeting with the Mother. If you recall, I was one of those people and I had told the story five years ago on my last trip to Auroville. The committee was preparing to offer a book of these stories for the upcoming Golden Jubilee of the 50th Anniversary of the grounding of the Supramental Light. Mine was the final story to complete their book. They had been looking for me for some time. My friend, the headmaster, invited two people to meet with me and we completed the story for the book entitled, *Darshan*.

After offering the manuscript of my book on Sri Aurobindo's Darshan, and after I had said goodbye to the headmaster, I took a taxi from Pondicherry to my guest house in Auroville. When we arrived, I jumped out of the taxi, laid the book on a table, and looked through my purse for rupees to pay the driver. An Italian gentleman (my age), was sitting at the table. As the taxi drove away, he said, "This has your name on it."

I looked at him and smiled because we had become friends while living across from each other and eating our meals together at the guest house. I said, "I'm writing a book."

He picked it up, smiled, and said, "I would like to read it."

Smiling back, I said, "OK" I felt pleased with the prospect of his reading my work because this was a very educated man and, over the past few weeks, I had learned to respect his point of view.

A few days later, while we were sitting together eating breakfast he asked me if he could make a copy of my book. Surprised at the request, I asked, "Why?" He explained that every year in Milan he gave a series of lectures and he would like to use my book for new ideas. He saw the confused look on my face. Again I asked, "Why?"

He could see that I wanted to know what there was in the book that would interest him. He said, "You are a bridge."

I asked, "What does that mean?"

His answer was, "You are the Antahkarana." I asked him to spell the word. With a very Italian-like gesture, I turned both palms up in the air as if to say, "So!" He just smiled and said nothing. I requested him to e-mail his lectures to me in America. His answer was a smile. I later looked in a deluxe, three-inch thick dictionary for the meaning of the word "Antahkarana." It wasn't there, but the computer gave this definition:

Alice A Bailey – Antahkarana: There are three principal components that together constitute the bridge of the antahkaran. These are: 1) the life thread (or "sutratma"); 2) the consciousness thread; and 3) the creative thread…

The antahkarana is a bridge or line of communication that is gradually constructed within a being of the creative entity – from personality to monad. It opens the way for the creative energies of the entity to flow down through its various levels of consciousness. The bridge enables the entity to influence its physical manifestation (and environment), in a spiritually, consciously, and intelligently purposeful way. This goal is achieved when all the organisms living within (i.e. composing and expressing) the being of the creative entity are themselves willing and able to receive the creative influx from their "logos."

Also, they must be collectively and harmoniously aligned in their effort to fulfill the divine purpose.

Essentially, then, in the building of the rainbow bridge, a creator is required to bring the microcosmic lives that constitute His body of manifestation into conscious communion and cooperation with His spiritual creative will.

The antahkarana is called the "rainbow bridge" because it's composed of a seven-fold spectrum of microcosmic living forms. These forms exist within the being of their macrocosmic creator and must be brought into perfect alignment and focus before His spiritual/creative purpose can be fulfilled. The casual body of every human being vibrates to one of seven basic frequencies and, in time, we become consciously attuned to that vibration and, thus, also to the planetary logos who is its parent source. We then proceed to attune ourselves to our monadic vibration, so as to contribute our own brilliantly colored filament to the collective sevenfold "bridge of Light" that stretches between humanity and the creative consciousness of the solar logos.

In October, before leaving America, I had e-mailed my book to the gentleman from New England who was the speaker at the AUM conference. This was the man who had said he would like to read the book and maybe direct me to a publisher. After Christmas vacation, he e-mailed me. His message was, "I finished your book. It is good. You need a copy editor to clean up some small stuff, but the content is good." He told me to publish it and he would help me find a publisher.

I was jubilant because this was the first person to respond after having read the manuscript and l had a high regard for his opinion. More than that, he was a person who was very involved with Sri Aurobindo and the Mother, and his knowledge of Their work was extensive. He had explained about my central question, "Why the red letters and the date on my small packet from the Mother?" He said, "The date is the date that Mother extracted the hostile entity from your body, making that your real, spiritual birthday – or at least rebirth day. So that day represents for you the birth of Divine Love in the physical being; the day of the Mother's incarnation in the cells of your body." I can't, in words, fully express the gratitude I felt for this man. For once, someone believed that this could really happen. Every other person I had talked to about having the Mother's cells in my body had looked at me as if I were a bit delusional.

There is more to this story. When one of the committee members from the people making the book entitled *Darshan*, about the Sunday afternoon series of stories, read about this blessing packet with the red letters, she sent me a copy of a page of an Ashram book. It read, "On the occasion of Kali Puja in 1972, Mother gave Divine love blessing packets to all. It was on 5.11.1972 (the date of my red letter packet with Her picture). She distributed them freely."

I e-mailed this page to New England. He replied, "A very interesting document. Kali Puja makes sense, as she is the destroyer of adverse forces. But, furthermore, this document suggests that there was some sort of breakthrough on that day that Mother was aware of. So your individual rebirth may have been part of a larger collective action. Interesting."

My reaction: The day the Mother pulled the body, which I felt was ugly, from my back was two days before Kali Puja. My name was posted on the board in large, capital, red letters on Kali Puja (5.11.1972). That was the date when M.P. Pandit had said the Divine had descended. The friend from Massachusetts had said, "Mother must have been aware of..." These words made me joyful because, if that were the case and the Divine had descended in me on that day, The Mother would have known of the completion of this action before she left her body in 1973.

Lesson Eighteen – "Bring me the Book!"

I hadn't seen my friend, the Ashram Ayurvedic doctor, for five years. We had known each other since 1972. Meeting him again after so long an absence was a very pleasant encounter. I had the manuscript with me because I had written about him and I wanted him to OK what I had said. Two weeks later we met again. He said, "While I waited for you to arrive, I asked Mother to give me the meaning in your book of the time you danced and stomped your feet. The answer that came was, 'The bandages that bound her were cut like with a scissors and Divine Love entered her heart.' She said you were dancing with Divine Joy." I agreed because it certainly was a joyous occasion. He and I would soon have many discussions about other events that were mentioned in the book.

An Aurovillian friend took me to an Ashram doctor who had practiced medicine in America for many years. His specialty was the immune system, and my friend thought he might cast some light on my situation with the cancer nodes. She informed me that he was a very interesting doctor because he was also a medical intuitive.

He had three assistants that were usually seated behind him observing his work. We went into his office and my friend introduced me to everyone. She stayed throughout the interview. The doctor's first words to her as he held my hands to feel my vibrations were, "She is a very spiritual person. She doesn't need to be here at the Ashram because the Mother is with her wherever she goes." We talked about the cancer, and his comment was, "Don't worry, it's not a threat. Come back in a week with your health records and we will look at them more closely." My friend showed me his donation box. I found some rupees and we left.

A week later I returned. He checked my records and told me not to worry about the cancer. He took hold of my upper arm, the one that in Spain had given me so much trouble, and he said, "Let's take care of this muscle." He squeezed it hard. That action gave me confidence in his intuitive ability because I hadn't mentioned my bad arm. He went quiet, and while concentrating in silence stepped into another mindset. He said, "You are afraid of a relationship with a man because of what you have suffered with your husband. You need a companion in your life." (Not him; he wasn't flirting.)

I laughed and said, "That isn't possible because whenever I get involved with a man, I can read his mind (only when his action is a threat to me), and that is the end of the relationship. I can't seem to find a man who is open, trusting, honest, and not afraid." I was dead serious. He gave a belly laugh. I said, "If you are interested in more unusual things about me, you can find them in a book I am writing."

He said, "Bring me the book." I dropped it off the next morning.

I had moved from Auroville to Pondicherry because the skin around my eyes was inflamed. That happened because every morning a teacher from the school dropped his son off at a Day Care Center near the guest house where I was staying, and he would pick me up and give me a ride to school on the back seat of his motorbike. The roads in Auroville weren't paved, and when a car or motorbike passed, we were engulfed in a cloud of dust and red dirt flew into my face (I now wear transparent goggles). I had been to the Ayurvedic doctor with my red, watery eyes and he suggested I move into Pondicherry near the Ashram.

Once I had moved in, I had another problem because the new guest house could only give me a fifteen day reservation. The New Year holidays had just finished and January and February are the busiest season of the year. To make matters worse, I had just extended my stay in India because I learned about the Ashram's special 50th Golden Jubilee Anniversary. I had to find other places to stay until March 15th, but for now, I had fifteen days in Golconde, the Mother's most treasured guest house. I was happy because I would be able to eat all of my meals in the Ashram dining room. Three days a week I took a taxi to and from the school in Auroville.

Once again, an incident with my book occurred. I figured all this activity with the book was because I had offered it to Sri Aurobindo. Ever since then, the book seemed to have a path of its own. On this day, the headmaster had returned my manuscript and I had laid it next to my briefcase on a stone bench in the lobby of the school. The new, young, teacher who drove to and from work with me had walked into the open aired room and was standing next to me, while I was sitting on the bench. We were ready to leave for the day. He said, "Is this yours? It has your name on it."

That night he read the book. The next morning he returned it and said nothing. After school he asked me if he could take it home to read it again. The following morning he said, "You wrote that book for me. We are going to work together. We are going to work for the Mother." His only aim in life is to be an example of a human who has given up his animal nature in order to transform into a spiritual being. He has completely surrendered his life to do work of the Mother. As he handed me the book, he looked seriously into my eyes and said, "The Mother knows the path. You are like a child riding on Her shoulders. She knows the target, She has the gun and you are the bullet."

…"human beings come into a physical body without knowing why, most of them go through life without knowing why, they leave their body without knowing why, and they have to begin the same thing all over again, indefinitely, until one day someone comes along and tells them, "Be careful! you know, there is a purpose to this. You are here for this work, don't miss your opportunity!" And how many years are wasted."

Collected Works of the Mother - 8:176

Lesson Nineteen – The Cleansing

Around ten days after I was in Golconde Guest House, I woke up at four o'clock in the morning. What occurred that night came without warning, "What is happening to me?" I thought I was going to pass a small amount of gas and instead I soiled my bed. It was unexpected because I was feeling fine. I quickly got up to go to a bathroom located about a hundred yards down the hall. After filling a pail with lukewarm water and soapsuds, I hurried to my room to clean my bed. As I started to rub the sheets, it felt like a volcano had erupted inside of me.

Vomit shot out of my mouth into the pail I was washing with. (It was like the force that caused me to vomit when the Mother pulled the body out of me.) As fast as it came out of my mouth, it came out of my behind. The force of each action was simultaneous and completely unexpected. I stood there in amazement, not knowing what was happening. I turned to clean up the floor and felt that I had to vomit again, so I ran down the hall to the bathroom. I didn't know how to react. In a dripping nightgown, I staggered back to my room. I got some of my towels and began to clean up the mess. Soon I was vomiting again. This action of vomiting and diarrhea went on for some time.

I was hopelessly not in control of caring for myself. Luckily, my neighbor was a friend of mine. I quietly knocked on her door and asked for help. She got up and didn't know where to begin. Should she clean me up first or the smelly floor? Each time I thought it was over, it started up again. Eventually, she was able to make me a clean bed because I always carry sheets with me when I travel.

My friend gave me some wash up cloths, one of her dressing gowns, and a clean blanket. By the time the dirty clothes were in a pile in the hall and I was ready to go back to bed, I couldn't fathom what had happened or was happening. The whole episode took over an hour and a half. By the time I finished vomiting, only clear water was coming out of both ends of me. It seemed as if someone had lifted the top of my head open and water was being poured down through my body. I felt like a gushing, leaking, cracked teapot. Once I was quietly in bed and thinking back on what had happened, I realized I had been cleansed.

Years ago in Princeton, New Jersey, as a part of a yoga program, I had gone through a water cleansing. On that day, at nine o'clock in the morning, I began to flush out my body by drinking a large glass of warm salt water. Then I was to begin a series of specific exercises, go to the bathroom, drink more water, and exercise again. I monitored my urine until it was clear and grains of sand were visible to the eye. Now, the instructor could know that my cleansing was complete. This night, while calmly tucked in my bed, I felt the same way; I had been cleansed. My body had experienced the force of the higher chakras as they encountered the cleansing force of the lower chakras.

After this episode, I stayed in bed for two days because I had no appetite and absolutely no strength left. The next Tuesday was the 50th Golden Jubilee of the Supramental Golden Light descending on earth. In the morning, I was to go to the Mother's room with the teachers, school children and their parents. We were to meet in the courtyard of the Samadhi.

It was a glorious day at the Ashram. Ashramite women were dressed in colors of white and gold, or clothes trimmed with gold. The men wore their best white outfits. Everyone looked neat, pressed, and happy. The Mother's meditation room had golden curtains draped from the ceiling to the floor. Beautiful arrangements of flowers lined the walkways and filled the room. I was glad that I had changed my airline ticket so I could put on my golden-trimmed, Indian dress and witness this very special celebration.

While sitting on a bench waiting for the group from the school to arrive, two members of the committee who compiled the stories about the Mother came to sit next to me. They had just come from the Mother's Room, where they had offered their book, *Darshan* to Her. I would be the first one to see the book after they had offered it. They joyfully placed a copy in my hands. The wife of the man said, "You got a good number in the book."

I looked for my story, and it was Chapter 18. Later, I asked the young teacher the significance of number eighteen. He said, "It means New Birth."

The following day at school, I began limping. With each hour that passed, it got worse. The next morning I went to the office of the medical intuitive doctor. I walked into his room, he held out his hands, and said, "How is my most interesting patient?" I groaned. He said my problem was a sciatic nerve. He put me face down on a table and gave me a back treatment, which helped.

He had finished my book and was impressed with my spiritual progress. He was especially interested in the battle with my mind. He told me I had learned to monitor my own thoughts and that was no easy task. He went on to say, "You are an Indigo child. Do you know what that means?" I shrugged my shoulders and said that I had a slight idea. I knew that the Mother had said that children who were born after 1967 were Indigo children. They had a new level of consciousness. I asked myself how he could be talking about me because I was seventy-five years old. Then I remembered that I had been reborn in 1967! It was an intimate moment.

I felt free to tell him something I had only told one other person. I talked about the time that Sri Aurobindo came to me in Barcelona. I said, "I know that the heated disk that descended on me was a golden disk. I couldn't see the color because it came from above my head, but my intuition had been very strong. Later, in my reading, I came across a statement from, as

I recall, either the Reg Veda or the Upanishads that talked about a golden lid being lifted. I explained that, a few days ago, I had read *The Yoga of Transformation*, by M.P. Pandit. In chapter 7, I found:

"Above the Overmind there is a famous golden lid, beyond which is the higher hemisphere, beginning with Vijnana or the Supermind. A fissure, an opening, has to be made in the lid above the head. The action of the ascent, aspiration, is seconded by a powerful descent from above. This joint action of the ascent and the descent splits open the lid and there is a downpour of this highest Truth-Consciousness."

He smiled, gave me some pills, and told me to try to sleep on my side with a pillow between my legs.

In the hotel, I moved to a room that had a tub. I thought soaking my leg in hot water might help relieve the pain. It didn't. That night taking three baths, my leg on a pillow, and pills didn't relieve the nerve–racking pain. The constant throbbing was as severe as the vibration of an inflamed tooth.

It was now March and rooms in guest houses were not filled, so trying a new place in Auroville away from the dusty roads, I thought, would be safer for my sensitive eyes. Before I left, I saw the doctor again. When he finished, he sat me in a chair in front of him. He gave me a special card that everyone had received when they visited the room of the Mother on the day of the Golden Jubilee. It had a picture of golden swans. He said, "These are the wings that came to you in Barcelona."

My bags were packed, so I took a taxi to Auroville and a new guest house. At dinner on the third evening, the pounding pain was intensifying. An American woman my age looked at me and said, "My dear, you have tears in your eyes. You look like you are ready to cry. You need much stronger pain pills. My father was a doctor, and I have a prescription for the strongest pain pill that I know." The woman seated next to her offered to buy them for me the following day when she went into Pondy.

The children and staff at Isai Ambalam School were having a goodbye party for me. The pain in my leg was bad, but there was no way I could disappoint them, so I went to the party anyway. I was so happy I hadn't missed the fun, as it turned out to be some of the most cherished moments of my life. As the party started, they led me to a chair that was placed in the middle of an open, double doorway. I was told not to move and not to look up. The girls came with flowers for my hair. That was a daily routine. Boys and girls would always bring flowers to offer to the Mother during the school's morning meditation. Of those flowers, they would select some that matched my dress and pin them in my hair. They would put a matching bindi on my forehead which would be placed in the area above the eyes.

When the headmaster entered the room and sat down, the party began. A boy came over and pulled a cord above my head, and petals of flowers fell over my body. One by one, the children came up with gifts. Most of them were handmade, beaded pieces like rings, arm and leg bracelets, earrings, and necklaces. The girls painted my nails with nail polish and made designs with henna on my hands. I received lipstick and eye brow pencils (which made one feel young). The teachers also gave me many thoughtful gifts.

The party was a very special tribute from them to me. The children bought money from home for cookies and drinks. They bought Seven-Up, instead of Coke (which they all liked more), because that's what I liked to drink. I was weakened and deeply touched because of the way they lovingly honored me. Returning to this school, the children, the teachers, and the headmaster for the past five years has become an important event for someone my age. As a side note, let me tell you that the teachers told me that when I left for home a year ago and an airplane flew over the playground, the entire school of over 100 kids in unison called out, "Goodbye, Shirley!" SUCH SWEETNESS! How does one stand it!

At eight o'clock the next morning, it was time to leave. I had cut off the lower part of the egg crate foam to use so I could soften the airplane seat for the long ride home. When I sat down in my aisle seat, I wasn't very happy. A large man whose arm was going to spill over into my arm rest was seated in the window seat next to me. I thought, "Oh boy, this is going to be an ordeal, a ten hour ride in squeezed quarters."

The hostess came and told him to fasten his seat belt. He said, "There is no seat belt!"

After a few minutes of searching, she said, "You're right, you'll have to move. You can't sit in a seat without a belt."

To myself, under my breath, I said, "Am I hearing this correctly? YES! HURRAH! It's going to be a two-seater ride home." The Mother must have prepared the way because from Paris to America, another 10 hour ride, I had three seats in the back row. I laid out my egg crate, made a bed, and swallowed pain pills every four hours.

When I turned the key in the door of my apartment, my neighbor walked past. By the shocked look on her face, I could tell what I looked like. My good friend, Abbie, brought me food and the next day took me to the grocery store. She then stayed away until I was ready to come out of hiding.

I called an Orthopedic doctor for an appointment and had to wait ten days. After five more days of rocking and walking, I couldn't see any improvement. I was beginning to get like a crazed woman. It had been over twenty-one days without a good night of sleep. I took my large picture of the Mother in my hands and we had a long talk. When I first met the Mother, I got the distinct message that She couldn't use me to do Her work if I didn't have my emotional self under control.

When that throbbing began again at nine o'clock that night, I had had it. I broke down and cried. I was 75 years old and I had been fighting the asuric (adverse) forces for five years of continuous roadblocks while writing this book. I said that She was expecting too much of me. I told Her I could continue to do

Her work, but later, after I had a good rest. Instead of holding Her picture, I should have read a book to remind me of Her suffering while changing the cells in Her body. She had to get to the mind of the cells in order to transform them and they weren't ready to help. My pain next to Hers was nothing. I was feeling remorseful because I had given in to my emotional–vital mind.

Lesson Twenty – The Rainbow Bridge

At the beginning of the war in Iraq, among other fears, I became concerned about the articles that were taken from the rooms in the museum in Baghdad. I had once read there were over one thousand Sumarian tablets that still had not been deciphered and I wondered if they had been there when the place had been ransacked. I thought to myself, "You have been all over the world, but still have not visited the bedrock of early Christian civilizations. You had better hurry before it's too late and everything is destroyed!" I had been interested in that mysterious land ever since my grandfather had read me Bible stories about the Phoenicians, Babylonians and Hittites.

I knew that I had to push myself, just one more time, to make an effort to take an adventurous trip somewhere in that vicinity. Otherwise, I wouldn't have felt that I had completed my trips around the world. For years, dreaming of going to Turkey was a part of my yearly travel plans, but, at my age, I was not interested in going by myself and was not very interested in taking a tour.

As if someone had read my mind, a brochure from a group of people with whom I had spent three days at a conference arrived in the morning mail. One of them, the director of a Mystery School (a Walk-In), was organizing an excursion to Turkey. The chances of going seemed slim, because I had already purchased an airline ticket to Spain and would be in Barcelona during that trip. Also, two weeks in Turkey during the middle of August would be hot. It gets to more than ninety degrees in the shade.

I was stewing in my mental juices because I really wanted to join them, but I felt I might slow down the pace of the group. Then I recalled that the woman leading the group was seventy years old, and she had led groups to this country on three earlier occasions. I thought, "If she can climb over rocks of ruins in the hot sun, so can I. This might be my last opportunity to travel on a pilgrimage with like-minded people."

Arrangements were made so I could fly from Barcelona to Istanbul, where I would join the group before their plane took off for Ankara, the capital of Turkey. We were to take along at least four white outfits because we were to meditate in various historic religious sites as we traveled the back roads of the land. As we drove through village after village, I kept thinking, "This view in front of me must look something like Iraq before they were invaded." My heart sank as I thought of the war and destruction of their lives.

Every morning while traveling to our daily destination, we would meditate for half an hour. I began to notice that the leader was finishing each meditation with the same series of sentences, always using the same group of words which had a rhythm of their own.

Halfway into the trip, we stayed at a spa near the Mediterranean Sea. We were to have a day and a half of R and R with sulfur mud baths, and, if you wanted, a Turkish massage. (I wanted, and it was wonderful, but I was ready to collapse in bed when it was over.) We arrived at our hotel in the early afternoon and everyone, before and after dinner, took a swim. The following day, for many hours, the entire group lounged around, covered with wet, sloppy, mineral mud. We then took turns having a massage. When I took my evening shower before hitting the bed, I was ready to drop, and drop I did! I threw myself on the bed still wrapped in my bath towel. The lights in the bathroom and my room were on because I thought that I would rest for a few minutes and then put on my gown, brush my teeth, and hit the hay.

What hadn't crossed my mind was the fact that I was on the ground floor, with a balcony that had a glass door to my room. Earlier in the day, I had washed out a cosmetic bag because some hand cream had leaked all over my things. I had put it in the sun on the balcony and, before the shower, went out to see if it was dry. I was exhausted and forgot to lock the door when I came back into the room. Without planning on it, after the shower, I fell fast asleep with the door unlocked, the lights on, the curtains not closed, and with only a towel covering my body.

At around four o'clock in the morning, I was awakened. I was lying on my stomach. While half awake and in a daze, I turned and saw a European male body, clad only in swimming shorts, leaving my room through the balcony door. The odor in my room was repulsive, the worst smelling male perspiration I had ever experienced. It was a sickeningly, rancid, horrific smell! I felt nauseous!

I had to clear the air, so without thinking of my safety, I ran to the door, looked outside, and saw nobody was in sight. So, safe or not, I quickly opened the doors and windows to air out the room. Getting rid of that smell was all I could think of. I lit some incense, turned on the overhead fan, and sat on the bed. A spot on my lower back felt as though it had been rubbed. I thought it was probably from a penis! I wondered if what I smelled was sperm. I didn't want to feel my back. I looked around my room. My passport, billfold, and money were still on the dresser, and my gold earrings and necklace were on the bed stand. He hadn't been interested in robbing me!

When the room had been aired out (I sprayed perfume near the fan), and when I felt safe, I closed the windows, locked the door, showered, and scrubbed myself with sandalwood soap. I opened the sheets on the clean bed next to me and meditated for the next hour. I asked the Mother to please remove all of the negative vibrations that I had experienced. I felt Her vibration slowly descend through the top of my head and spread throughout my body to cleanse me. Soon I was feeling my old self again. The trauma of the experience had ended, and I was cleansed and ready to, once again, enjoy my trip.

The next morning, at breakfast, I scoured the dining room looking to see if I could identify the man. I felt that I had to mention what had happened to me to our tour guide so he could warn the hotel. He, in turn, informed the leader of our tour. When I boarded the bus, she was informing everyone about the incident because she wanted to alert them to be more cautious for the remainder of the journey.

A full day trip on the bus began with the announcement that this was an auspicious day, because August 15 was the birth date of two famous religious people. I added, "It also is the birthday of Sri Aurobindo!" As soon as those words left my mouth, I realized that what had happened to me at four o'clock in the morning was on His birthday. I thought, "Oh my God! Last night happened on His birthday! This has to be some kind of special message from Him to me. Something very, very, important! What can it mean?" The tour leader led us in the regular morning meditation, and, as always, ending with the same set of words.

Ten minutes after she finished reading and as we settled into our seats, a young man who worked with her at the Mystery School came over to sit with me. I realized he had come to console me. I told him I was fine and explained how I had calmed myself down while meditating with the Mother. We had another hour of small talk, and when we finished, he opened a book. I casually asked him what he was reading, and he said, "The Rainbow Bridge."

Flabbergasted, I inquired, "Is that the same as the Antahkarana?"

He said, "Yes," I told him I had looked everywhere for that book. I begged him to let me take it to my room that night so I could read it. He happily agreed. I went to bed early and devoured the book.

The following day, I asked if I could buy it from him at the end of the trip. His answer was negative because it was a library book that belonged to the Mystery School. Later he said that

I could ask the leader to sell it to me and she did. I couldn't believe my good luck. I had been looking for information about Alice Bailey and the meaning of the antahkarana ever since I was first told about it six months earlier.

What I learned in the book was shocking, but not upsetting, because this had happened on the birthday of Sri Aurobindo. That fact verified, for me, that I was at the right place, at the right time, and with the leader of the group who was doing what needed to be done in order for me to progress along the spiritual path. I found the words she read each day on the bus to end our meditation came directly from the book. They were a great invocation or mantram of unification.

As I read about STAGE I of this initiation, it resonated with what had happened to me that night in Golconde, when I felt that I had been cleansed. As I now see it, before the rainbow bridge can be crossed, a force of a whirlwind of energy that comes from the Higher Light, which is located above the head, must do its work in the body. It is called STAGE I because the energy lowers itself (when the body is ripe), in layers of varied intensities of colors, to form a channel where the soul can push its force into the physical being. The energy forcefully flows from the top of the head to cleanse down through the middle of the body, where it deposits spent vibrations. These vibrations meet a surging force from below. I feel this is what happened to me in Golconde when I felt like a cracked teapot.

Now in Turkey, on August 15, Sri Aurobindo's birthday, as far as I was concerned, I was experiencing STAGE II (which was also explained in the book). The next step that is necessary before one can begin to cross the rainbow bridge is to remove thoughts from this and past lifetimes. These individual thoughts are caught in a huge bubble (cage) which is attached to the area on top of each human being's head. The removing of these energies of collected clouds of thought is accomplished when an animal-man opens the cage (pictured in the book) and the bubble explodes. A horrid smell escapes as the rotted thought forms are released. At last I knew what that putrid smell was! I needed to be thankful for the man (animal-man) who visited me in my room that night. I also needed to acknowledge that the leader of the group from the Mystery School was performing an initiation. I was being initiated and wasn't aware of it.

The book was just what I had been looking for and I am grateful to the authors. It introduced me to information which would more fully help me understand the function of the Antahkarana or Rainbow bridge. This may sound preposterous, but soon after I arrived back in Auroville, I experienced a serendipitous event. I selected two new books at the book store. The first was *Sri Aurobindo, His Life Unique*. It read, "He (Sri Aurobindo), had to prepare a rainbow bridge between earth and heaven."

The second book, *The Mother – A Short Biography*, stated, "It was here, on the ground of matter, the deeply buried Divine showed a golden seam which the Mother started pulling, as it were, in order to link spirit and matter, the two ends of the Divine."

To me, it doesn't seem strange (the pulling of the strings), that I just happened to choose these particular books to read right after I came home from Turkey, where STAGE II had happened. That is the way the Mother has led me ever since we first met. It is as if I am inwardly guided to what is Her next step on my agenda. On page 86 of *Sri Aurobindo, His Life Unique*, it had another startling statement. Sri Aurobindo had already written long ago in a letter, "The Supramental Consciousness will enter a phase of realizing its power in 1967." I reacted, "1967! That's when Sri Aurobindo came to me!"

Lesson Twenty one – Her Light

Like a caterpillar evolving, I know there will always be a next step with the Mother. I just wait silently, wrapped in my creative cocoon, for Her to make Her next move. I am going to close PART ONE of this book by relating a few new clues that have been revealed to me to let me know that my spiritual life is still inching along and that Her Light within me has taken on an intensity that I must become aware of.

A short time ago, I noticed more shining moments of Her love. It had to do with a new relationship with animals. I have never felt a need to have an animal. As a child growing up, we had hunting dogs but they lived in the barn. My mother did have a poodle for my children. In Africa we had an African gray parrot who was lots of fun and quite a talker, but it belonged to the children. I consider myself a non-animal person.

To my utter surprise, an unusual incident happened when I visited the home of my friend's daughter. She had a large boxer dog living in the house. After we had been seated for a short time, the dog came to me and laid his head on my bare feet. Her daughter laughed and looked surprised. She whispered, "He has never done that!" After lunch, we had coffee on the terrace and the dog came outside and put his head on my feet again. He stayed there for over an hour, until we left her house. The dog's owner called her husband into the house so he could see the dog in this position, saying he had to see this with his own eyes! I found it interesting and thought that the dog must be feeling the Mother's vibration.

Last month in London, while on the Underground, I sat next to a young blind man. His dog was on the floor next to him. Within seconds after I was seated, the dog raised himself up, turned around, put his paws on my knees, and placed his face on his paws. He was looking directly into my eyes. My son, who was standing next to me, knows that I feel uncomfortable around dogs and cats because they often give me fleas, so he immediately came to my rescue. He kindly placed the dog back resting on the floor. The dog quickly got up and repeated what he had done before. Everyone seated near us smiled because the dog had been on the floor, apparently not bothering anyone, until he saw me. The dog's eyes looked at me as if he were saying, "Please let me stay."

This time, I rubbed his face awhile and he remained there until it was time for one of us to leave. My granddaughter remarked, "That dog really loved you." The people on the Underground felt that way too. I felt it as well. That was a special moment with a special animal.

The next two stories happened four months ago while I was at Auroville. There was an Indian Dance Program at an open air auditorium, and I had gone there with two friends. As the performance ended, the Aurovillian (I could tell by the way she dressed), young, adult woman seated next to me (whom I didn't know), said as we got up to leave, "Thank you with your vibration for sitting next to me!"

Astonished, I said, "Could you feel my vibration?"

She said, "Oh, yes!" I ran into her the next day at the Auroville Café, she smiled a knowing smile, and went on her way.

The next bit of information happened the day before I left Auroville. Suzanne, a young, adult Dutch woman from the Center Guest House was also going to fly home the next day. We wanted to have our last meditation at the Matrimandir (the temple to the Mother at the center of Auroville), before leaving, so at 5 P.M. I hopped on the back of her motorbike and she took me with her to meditate. She sat under the banyan tree and I went into the temple.

Coming out and walking to the newly finished fountain located in the plaza of the temple, I ran into one of the men who had been in charge of the building. I said to him, "This is exquisite."

He said, "The Mother requires perfection." He was taking an Indian couple on a short tour and invited me to come with them. A young woman who had been sitting alone meditating when I first entered that space moved to come out of her meditation. As she did so, he asked her to join us. She got up, came over to me (a stranger), and lovingly held my face in her hands. She kissed me first on one cheek and then the other. We walked on to join the others.

The last and latest story is the best. I had been in the hospital again because the doctor thought I was having a stroke. A dentist had given me quite an ordinary pill when I had an abscessed tooth removed, and I reacted violently. My head went into a tailspin; I had vertigo, a pain in the arm and a high fever. After a few days, they found the left artery in my neck was seventy percent blocked. I had been in the hospital six days and had four doctors and their assistants working on me. They were puzzled because whatever medicine they gave me seemed to cause unusual reactions. I didn't dare mention the cells of the Mother because they would have thought that, in addition to all else, I was a bit loony.

One of the doctors who came in regularly was a neurologist. We happily shook hands twice a day. When it was nearing time for me to leave, I asked him if I needed to come to see him once I left the hospital. He said, "You can come to see me anytime because I will never forget you: not in three days, three months, or three years!" He walked out of the room. By the next time he came to my room, I had become curious, so I asked him why he wouldn't forget me. He replied, "I go in and out of rooms every day and I have done so for years. I have never seen anyone like you. There is a wide white light around your body." He firmly shook my hand and left the room.

I sat in bed half-smiling and half-serious because I knew the Light he had seen was the Mother's. The following day when he came in, I said, "I don't know what you saw, but whatever it was is a reflection of who you are. I am like a mirror."

He was overtaken with joy. He said, "That is so sweet!"

In this book I have placed before you what has been placed before me throughout this lifetime. I have put together the pieces of this puzzle as best I can. I have not always explained how I reacted to certain incidents and I'm sure you have, at times, been left hanging. My hope is that you would ask yourself what you would have done, if you had been in my shoes. I have made mistakes and have learned from them, so I hope not to have to repeat them in another lifetime. When Sri Aurobindo came to me in Barcelona, He said, "The agony of your life is over." Since that day, I have pondered the exact meaning of those words. My life has been complex and I have had to deal with it by myself. Fortunately, just after my thirty-seventh birthday, Sri Aurobindo came to my rescue and I am constantly reminded of His and the Mother's strength and force. The Mother reconstructed the cells of Her body to transform them for the emergence of a new Super-Spiritual Being. It took years of suffering in Her body.

Sri Aurobindo prepared the way and the Mother accomplished the goal of bringing down a new Light for the transformation into a better life for every human. All levels of consciousness will benefit from Her extraordinary gift to each of us. I know She has forgiven my moments of weakness and, with this book, I hope to help Her with Her mission of transformation. Her love and smiling face is always available. She is probably blessing each one of you as you read these pages.

The next chapter will be a short Intermission. As you read it, you will be able to see why I wrote this book. People kept telling me to write a book and I had to make sure that the Mother wanted this story told. In PART TWO you will find chapters explaining the process She used in order to help me develop spiritual awareness.

PART TWO - Reflections and Insights

Intermission

For years, many people had been telling me that I should write a book about my experiences while living and teaching in countries around the globe. I had one reply, "There is only one book to write and that is about my relationship with the Mother." One day in my morning meditation, I said to the Mother, "If you want me to write a book about all of the things that have happened since I have surrendered, you will in your own way, please, have to make me aware of it because my ego does not need to write a book. If You want a book, it will be Your book, because without You, I have nothing to write about."

After breakfast, while leaving my apartment, I walked down the outside stairs, where I met a neighbor who had an apartment for sale in our building. She was coming up the stairs with a potential buyer. My neighbor introduced me as a world traveler who spent most of her time in Spain. She informed me that Annie, the woman at her side, was from Romania. We exchanged small talk and I went on my way.

In the evening when I returned home, slipped under my door was a note from Annie. She had invited me for lunch so we could discuss the pros and cons of living in Spain. Two days later, we met at an open air restaurant on the ocean. She had been waiting since the place opened for lunch. She was sitting at a table, knitting. During our meal, there were many empty tables, so we didn't feel rushed. After a few hours of conversation, she said, "Your attitude toward living overseas is very different from most Americans. You should write a book!"

I told her I was thinking of writing a book, but it wouldn't be about living overseas. She wanted to know what my book would be about. When I finished telling her my story about Sri Aurobindo and the Mother, she held my hand and sincerely expressed an interest in typing the manuscript. She explained that she was a retired secretary and would love a project to work on. I informed her that most of the information was on cassettes. That didn't dampen her spirit, and she repeated that she was a professional secretary with years of experience and could do anything. I was hesitant to make a commitment because I still wasn't sure of what the Mother wanted of me. Annie left and while driving home I kept thinking, "Is the fact that a stranger appeared at my doorstep and offered to type the manuscript enough of a confirmation to write the book?"

As I readied myself for evening meditation, I happened to see the calendar. It was February 21, the Mother's birthday! I smiled, and shouted with glee. She had given me Her answer! I said, "OK, Mother, I got your message. You want a birthday present. I'll write the book!" It was Her day and someone had offered to type the book. The Mother had given me the sign I had been looking for. Now it was up to me. Annie couldn't wait and, soon after our conversation, she went to live in Italy.

Creative Incubation

Creative Incubation, what is it? To me, we are born with previously recorded, colored vibrations that one day will become White Light. I believe in reincarnation. Our DNA is only a part of who we are. These color-coded vibrations are us. I think of them as our cocoons because we are snuggled inside of them and they are snuggled inside of us. We are all different because our evolutionary growth has been individual, so the recording inside of our cocoons cannot be the same as our neighbors. Not even the same as our parents.

We are tied to matter, our physical bodies prove that. We are slaves to our physical, desire-emotional, and mental minds (They each have their own aspect of mind.) In our cocoons, we incubate and, unless we get creative, that evolutionary mass of color-coded, vibrating cells that are resonating within our bodies is not going to make a significant change. We need to help it along, or lifetime after lifetime we will make little progress. We need to dare, to dare to try new things. Why do we need to step out from the known to the unknown? Because we want more, we want to expand our vibrations. We want to refine them. We want to stimulate them so we can absorb more of the frequency of White Light.

We need to become brave enough to find the courage to leave the familiar to enter the unfamiliar. When you step out of order, you enter chaos. Balance is necessary in our lives, so in chaos we search for order in our new adventure. Once the adventure begins, step-by-step we slowly restore our confidence. When it is established, we gain the courage to dare to step into chaos again. We must take the first step, even though it may be a small one.

I am the only one who can change me, and you are the only one who can change you. How do we begin? We begin with truth. We must be true to ourselves and reverent to truth that surrounds us. It does surround us. We must look for the positive in life. Like attracts like, or you could say Light attracts Light. Change yourself and you change the world. When we change, we shake up matter. See how powerful we are! We can energize everyone around us.

Our thoughts are powerful. They are streams of energy. We are responsible for every thought that comes out of our head. My question to you is, "What are you, as one individual, adding to life?" My wish is that you are creative and adding joy. I hope I am doing the same. I didn't mean to give a lecture. I just wanted to bring to your attention the importance of stepping out and doing your own thing.

The real test of, "Put your money where your mouth is," came to me in the dream when I could have gone into the little cottage for love and security, but instead I chose to step into the unknown. I dared to dare. From that day forward, my motto was, "I would rather say, 'I'm sorry, I tried,' instead of 'I wish I would have.' Don't for one moment think I'm saying it is easy. It isn't, it takes courage, because no matter how hard you try not to, you are going to make mistakes. If no one loves you after you make a mistake, you have to be prepared to love yourself, for them and for yourself, and sometimes learn to say, "I'm sorry."

Giving up "me" in 1972 when I surrendered to the Mother was never a part of my plan. I still needed my ego. (At that time, I didn't know giving up your ego was the plan for spiritual growth.) She did not walk into my body. My creative self would never allow someone to completely change my style. The most exciting aspect of life is creativity and to be creative you need to be free. When I am lost in painting, I am extended in space for hours. The feeling is as good as a flying dream. I have told you about my devotion to the Mother. That never wavered. Now I want to tell you about my devotion to the creative side of my incubation.

Many years ago, when I first read the small book, *The Hundredth Monkey*, I inwardly flipped! Everything inside of me shot into second gear. Stepping out to do your own thing seemed normal! I could be monkey number one or monkey number one hundred, or any number in between. The thought of it immediately made me responsible for every action that I performed in life. Either you started something or you kept it going. The only thing that really mattered was that you were doing something to make the world a better place to live in.

For those of you who do not know the story, my short version is this: Scientists were feeding sweet potatoes to a group of monkeys on an island. One day, one of the young, female monkeys took her potatoes to the water to wash them. After some days, she was joined by her mother and other young females. It wasn't long before all of the young monkeys were washing their sweet potatoes before they ate them. The adult monkeys became curious and they observed and copied the behavior of the younger monkeys. When the hundredth monkey followed suit, it set up a vibrational resonance to another island where scientists were feeding and observing monkey behavior. All at once, all of those monkeys began a new habit. They began to wash their potatoes. To me, this validated the Morphogenetic Fields Theory of Rupert Sheldrake and explained the creative aspect of evolution.

The importance of the concept of the hundredth monkey motivated me in everything I saw and touched. My aim was to steer my life in the direction of innovativeness, and deciding what that direction might be certainly wasn't easy. With this new inspiration, this new mental shot in the arm, in spite of the depressed situation in which I found myself, I began my daily, routine, life over again. When you are bogged down with responsibility, and have no money, it is hard to see the forest for the trees. Daily grind saps all of your precious energy. The trick is to breathe some fresh air into your existence. After a divorce, I began teaching all day and going to an art class once a week.

Fortunately, I did this at a graduate level university course. Some years later, with five or six classes completed, I realized that I was accumulating credits towards a Master of Fine Arts Degree. My final project was twenty-five watercolor paintings for a one woman show and an MFA.

In 1952, I had graduated from college with a teaching degree in art. I found those jobs few and far between, so I moved on to a MA in Reading. I had lived in Mexico, so I could speak enough Spanish to qualify to teach migrant education. My new job took me back to the Dutch town where I was raised. I fully understood the difference between the Mexican and Dutch cultures. I was content because I felt I was a bridge between these two groups of people. It was a matter of being at the right place at the right time.

A program offered by the National Diffusion Network in Washington, D.C., called, "Learning to Read through the Arts," was presented at one of our teacher's meetings. It was geared to help children who were turned off to reading. That was most of the migrant children, so a friend and I went to New York City to become certified trainers for the program.

We qualified because we had degrees in art and reading. It turned out to be one of the most innovative programs in the district. Our school received a grant to back a project for the migrant summer school. We chose a musical, the Wizard of Oz, because Frank Baum, the author of the book, had received some of his inspiration for the story while visiting a resort, Castle Park, which was located near us on Lake Michigan. We had field trips to the Castle, and the woman who inspired the character, Dorothy, came from Chicago to see the performance. At the parents' potluck supper, the children presented her with a heart pillow they had made. That program turned out to be a perfect public relations project for the school and migrant parents.

The importance of the vibrations set up by one individual monkey never left me. It gave me tremendous freedom. My aim was to develop plans for the most perfect possibilities for children to learn. I became assistant director of the summer program. We were the only group of children in the Summer School at that time, so we could concentrate on cultural issues in order to establish self-esteem. The result was a personal, academic, and creative program. We never measured our goals in relationship to other programs throughout the state. We did our own thing. If we were monkey number one, we were going to give it our best shot.

Apparently, we did it right, because in 1985 I was the first person in the state to receive the Michigan Education Association's Migrant Teacher of the Year Award. The icing on the cake happened when Luz Elena Muñoz nominated me for Who's Who of American Teachers. When one of your students honors you, it is the greatest complement you can receive and a great way to exit a career.

For sixteen years, while I worked in the school district, I kept asking the Mother if this work was Her work. I got my answer when I found out the address of the place where the migrant award was going to be held, in Detroit, and the number of the building was 1717. The number 17 is the number the Mother uses to let me know when it is a temporary situation. I retired and challenged myself to dare to write this book.

Fragmented color

For me, the object of life on earth is to fine tune our vibrations to receive and become White Light. That is my interpretation of the message I got when I was eleven years old. While I was seated in church, a voice came to me, saying, "Everyone is going to become A Jesus." Jesus was an enlightened being. That is what Christians believe and, at that time, I was a Christian. Since then, I have learned that most religions follow the influence of various enlightened beings.

The task of becoming enlightened seems an endless journey, but we must begin somewhere. When I met the Mother, I got a jump start. Searching four years for the mystery man, Sri Aurobindo, had opened my eyes to a world of new experiences. I was prepared to examine any new concept of what life had to offer. Yoga, which means union with the Divine, was the beginning of the search and surrender was the process. Each person has an individual path, and just because others were going in one direction, didn't mean that what they were pursuing was right for me. I felt I was alone in my search.

When you become aware that the effort is worth all the trials and tribulations you might encounter along the way, you make an earnest attempt to change. Sincerity is your ticket into yourself. My method was to ask my inner, color-coded guide (along with the Mother), to lead me in the right direction. Very slowly, I realized they had heard my call. Soon, situations that you would call coincidence began to happen. Someone would give me a book, fortune cookies would have a message, and some friends with new ideas would enter my life. I thanked the guide and the Mother for helping me. It is important to give thanks when you are given what you have asked for.

At a farm house in France, the direction of the search took a roundabout turn. I hazily woke up and looked out of an open window. There were no screens and the sun was shining brightly. It looked as if floating confetti was falling from the sky. I assumed it was particles of dust. My reaction was, "Wow, dust is multi-colored!" Weeks later, I was on an airplane flying above the water while landing in New York City. A reflection of colored confetti was sparkling across the waves. Sometime later, while driving my car in the sunshine, after a rainfall, I noticed that the tiny beads of water stuck on the windshield were a rainbow of reflections. The different colors that are connected with the chakras in the body came to mind. I thought, "Are we, and everything in nature, nothing more than color that is on a journey to become White Light?"

This new awareness changed how I viewed everything. I saw fragmented light everywhere. Thoughts and objects were nothing but fragmented light. Reading Sri Aurobindo and learning about the physical, vital, and mental minds, I pictured them all as color-coded vibrations. I visualized a mass of mixed up, colored spaghetti (the three minds), inside my head. How was I going to untangle this mess? First of all, I had to know what I was dealing with. I decided to give each of these minds a name so I could more fully become aware of how and when each of them was working.

Jane was the physical mind, Mary the vital (desire-emotional), and Clair was the mental mind. I watched them work and asked myself why they were doing certain things. Many times, they were working together. I figured if I could really get to know the action of one part of mind, I could separate it, and the other two would follow suit, like the resonance of the hundredth monkey.

Different degrees of fragmented colors! The concept was so simple. Sometimes the colors were not visual, but frequency auras around people, relationships, speeches, movies, animals, cities, countries, anything and everything. Turning those thoughts inward to reincarnation, I imagined a huge ball of multi-colored strands of wound up yarn or vibrating layers of lifetimes that you could peel like an onion.

A psychometrist holds a piece of jewelry that you have worn every day. He/she tells you about the details of your life because he/she can read the vibrations that are released from it. In New York City, many years ago, my daughter and I had separate sessions with a holy man from India. He released the locked-up, vibrating feelings inside our bodies. I realized the important thing for me to do was to get in touch with the inner me. I wanted to un-peel the layers of this lifetime.

Three years ago, my request was answered. It was Easter weekend. Thursday evening, a friend of mine had signed up to sit in church to cover a prayer vigil from four to five o'clock A.M. She asked me to join her because she didn't want to be alone at that early hour. The silence in the church was calming and it set me up for a worshipful weekend.

A unique Easter morning sunrise service was being held at an open-air restaurant on the ocean across the street from where I lived. I decided to attend the service. I wore a special white dress I had bought when I went to Chicenitza for a ceremony in Mexico. That occasion was the grounding of a five-hundred year old, Mayan prophesy. I felt the dress was full of spiritual vibrations. I looked a bit out of place in a white, peasant, marriage dress, but I figured, "Who cares?" I was familiar with the church service because Easter songs of my childhood were sung while we observed other church groups gather on the beach to baptize parishioners. After the service, most of the crowd stayed to have breakfast.

I was walking home through the parking lot as the friend who had invited me to the vigil the day before was leaving to go to church. She stopped the car and asked if I wanted to join her. I said, pointing to my Mayan outfit, "Dressed like this?"

She said, "Who cares?" That was the right answer. I stepped into the car and went to another church.

This service was a display of colorful pageantry. All ages of participants were wearing elaborate costumes. The church was full. This was the second service of the morning. As the procession began to come down the main aisle, it was ushered in by the use of flags and the sound of trumpets. The blasts were sharp, high pitched, and shrill. Chills ran up and down my spine. For a moment, my body trembled. The reaction was unusual. We returned home by noon.

As I sat on the balcony sipping tea, I realized something was radically wrong with me. What was it? I was half-crying and I didn't know why. I got up and walked around the room. I kept holding my head and saying, "Something is going to happen. I can feel it. Something is wrong!" I said it a dozen times. The feeling inside of me was like a tremendous wave was going to hit. An internal storm was brewing. I couldn't sit. I kept walking and repeating the same words.

I realized I was out of control. I called the woman I had gone to church with. She immediately came up to my apartment, saw my condition, and called a neighbor who was a nurse. The nurse tried to talk to me and calm me down.

As I tried to explain my feelings, I recognized I was consumed with an overwhelming fear that something was going to, or had, happened to my granddaughter. I was sure of it. My neighbor had me call my son in Mexico and he called my daughter in America. My daughter called to tell me that my three year old granddaughter was fine. I slowly calmed down, my friends left, and I went to rest on the bed.

I remained silent for some time. Then the reason for my behavior surfaced. I was reliving and releasing the pent-up emotions of the death of my first child. I wept uncontrollably. When it was over, I was amazed at how much sadness I still held onto, at how much feeling had not been liberated so many years ago when she had passed away.

The same type of release happened when I was writing in this book about the death of my brother. It was six o'clock in the morning and I wept for hours. At the time, I thought, "What a catharsis! Everyone should write a book." The good news was that I was learning to peel away old vibrations. I was unwinding with more and more clarity. The cleansing was making room for silence and calm throughout my body. I felt I was moving forward toward my goal of serenity.

The Lesson

Two days ago, I received photos of my cousin's new house. There were over 30 pictures with a map showing me each room at different angles. For weeks she had been telling me how excited she, her husband, and her daughters were about the new house. They wanted to live in it for the rest of their lives. Everything had been settled and they were ready to sign the final papers. I was excited too because she had found a nine-room house, on ten acres of land. The house had a pond and they could use it for swimming in the summer and ice-skating in the winter. There was enough space to have cross-country skiing trails. Everything seemed perfect. Unfortunately for her lovely family, I entered the picture.

I excitedly opened her packet of photos. The first few pictures were scenes of the car approaching a wooden house as you drove up a long, tree-lined driveway. The house was attractive. As I continued to look through the pictures, I became concerned because the house was exactly as it had been when it was built in the 1970's, and I thought it would need a lot of repair.

My cousin had told me that the original shag carpets were still on the floors, and they, in time, would need to be changed. She said the first carpet to go was one she described as puke green. We both laughed. I told her I remembered those times because I had that same color green car. As I viewed more pictures, I became more and more concerned. The kitchen and dining room had dark wooden cabinets. I froze in my tracks because I had just sold a house where I had the dark cupboards sanded and then painted, but the paint had cracked off. I ended up getting the whole kitchen redone, and it cost me $25,000.

Every hour, more or less, I would look at those photographs and I became fascinated with trying to understand what people had lived in that house. I figured you could tell a lot about the woman because of the drapes and curtains, but the man seemed to be a compulsively-driven handyman. Only a few walls in the whole house were not paneled.

My cousin had said they were going to pull up all the rugs, so, in the long run, this house would be fine. I am an artist; the use of color, contrast, and consistency in decoration is very important to me. As I looked at this house, I thought, "Who could live for thirty-five years in a house like this?" I looked again and again at all of the photographs. Every wallpapered area had a colored pattern. I said out loud in a strong voice, "This house is immaculately cared for, needs lots of work, and has great potential, but look at this puke green in the master bedroom. It is so ugly!" I went to bed.

Four, five, six hours passed and I was still wide-awake. Something was wrong, but what? I couldn't figure it out. There was such a buzz in my heart. A pressure of vibrations was so near me and it was constant. I couldn't figure out what was happening. I got up, walked around the room, and went back to bed. This happened the whole night. I didn't even know if I slept. But the thought, "ugly, ugly, so ugly" kept racing through my head. I couldn't clear my head long enough to wonder why I was saying it.

Morning came and I couldn't eat because my stomach was a churning of nerves. I was curled up in my bed in a fog of vibration. I felt helpless and stayed there holding myself until four o'clock in the afternoon. I finally had a light snack and went back to bed. At four-thirty I wanted to call to speak to my cousin's husband before she came home from work at five o'clock. I wanted to find out from him how many panels they were going to take down. I thought that with more information I would be prepared to talk to her.

All of this time, the words "ugly, ugly, ugly" were pouring into me. My head was a buzz, my heart was a buzz, and I was obsessed with the word "ugly." I couldn't get outside of myself long enough to observe myself, to find out why I was saying it. I had tried to shake it out of my memory. I meditated, but it was constantly there. I kept asking, "What is wrong with me?"

I wasn't ready to speak to my cousin, but I knew she would call after supper to ask about the photos, so I wanted to be ready. I wasn't alert enough to go out for the evening and not be home when she called. Doing that, I could have waited and called her the next day when things had calmed down. At four-thirty, I called her house and she answered the phone. My heart sorrowfully sank. She caught me off guard. I said to her, "I'm surprised you're at home. Why aren't you at work?"

She said, "It's a snow day, so we all came home at noon. Did you get the photographs?"

I said, "Yes, and I think that this house is going to own you."

She asked, "What do you mean?"

I answered "Well, as a child I lived in a house with a long driveway, and all winter long you had to get up early to plow the snow. Sometimes, if it snowed during the day, you had to walk to get the snowplow before you could clear the way to get your car into the driveway.

"The fact that you have two fireplaces, a wood stove, and steam heat means this house is hard to heat. The price of oil is going up and, because of demand, will never go down."

She stopped me and said, "You hate it!"

For a moment, there was silence. I knew that she had picked up from my mind, "Ugly, ugly, ugly!" I should have said, "No, I don't hate it," but I was afraid that the word "ugly" would come out of my mouth. I told her I had been up most of the night, was so upset, and couldn't eat food until four o'clock in the afternoon.

She made some remark like, "It sounds a bit extreme."

I said, "I just don't know what to say."

She said, "You could have said, 'I hope you will be very happy in your new home' or something like, 'I like your new house.' Couldn't you have faked it?"

I said, "I couldn't fool you; I have never lied to you. You would have known."

She said," I half-expected you would find something wrong." My mother in-law loved it."

I said, "I'm so sorry, I really want you to be happy."

I felt terrible. How could I be so hurtful to someone I dearly loved? After some moments of silence, she replied, "I know you always want the best for me." I hadn't expected to talk to her. She was a cousin who was like a sister. She had no brothers and sisters, and look what I was doing to our friendship. I really didn't say the right things at the right time. I felt lousy and unkind.

She said, "Well, we love a seventies house. We were very happy then.

I said, "Maybe that's what's wrong with me. That was the worst period of my life. I spent those years in a double-wide, seventies style, mobile home."

To end the conversation, she said, "We sign the papers in twenty-two days. Please send the pictures back; I want to send them to my friends."

When she hung up the phone, I thought, "She certainly is a mature woman. She really handled that well." I knew she put up a good front, but I was sure she went to her bedroom and cried.

I went to bed and tried to cry myself to sleep, but it just didn't happen. Two o'clock in the morning I was wide-awake and still not knowing what was wrong. The vibrations didn't stop and "ugly, ugly, ugly," was eating up my mind. I was so miserable and so, without knowing what to do, I got up, took a large picture of the Mother off of a shelf, looked into Her eyes, and said, "Please help me." I placed Her picture over my heart and, hugging it, went back to bed. I said to Her, "There is a major reason this is happening, because when my cousin answered the phone, instead of her husband, that was no mistake. What do you want to tell me? What is this all about? What do you want me to learn? Is this about love?"

Time passed; it silently passed. Slowly, I began to say, "Please don't buy the house. Please don't buy the house. Please don't buy the house." (Where did those words come from? I never thought of not buying the house!) "Please don't buy the house." In a forceful manner, the words kept falling from my mouth. I must have said it twenty times. All at once, my voice changed into a male voice. The voice mimicked me in a sing-song rhyme. It was a male imitating a female. Trying to act cutely, "P-l-e-a-s-e.. d-o-n-'t.. b-u-y.. t-h-e.. h-o-u-s-e.." It got more aggressive as it repeated over and over, each time louder and more adamantly, "PLEASE DON'T BUY THE HOUSE!" As it went on repeating, it got more and more out of control, more furious! Finally, in a rage, my lips curled and like a growl, it yelled, "PLEASE DON'T BUY THE HOUSE!" My hands were raised in a claw-like motion. I felt that this, whatever it was, wanted to tear me apart.

The night became silent once again. I had the covers pulled up to my neck. I listened, looked around, and said, "Was that the beast?" I listened to my inner self (my gut feeling), and said, "No the beast has more force than that and would never be out of control. That was an entity. That was an entity that is attached to that house. It is probably the man who worked so hard and loves that house so much. It probably got so upset when I said the word "ugly" that he had to pay me back. I had insulted his taste with my remarks. It was more than he could bear. How could anyone not love his precious house? When it heard, "Please don't buy the house," it became outraged. In the beginning, when I had only used the word "ugly" it was upset. I believe it wanted to torment me and, just like a mosquito that you can't catch, keeps annoying you, this entity kept buzzing me. It worked, because I certainly was confused. When the Mother entered the picture, She knew exactly what to do. She put the words "Please don't buy the house" into my mouth and that so enraged this entity that it exposed itself. There had to be more to this story because my cousin was too badly hurt.

When I got up the next morning, I realized that there was something wrong with this picture. My cousin loved the house. Her family loved the house. The entity loved the house. I was the one who didn't fit in. I knew there was a reason, a huge lesson for me to learn. My cousin wouldn't have been hurt so deeply for a superficial cause. I was reading a spiritual book called *The Tree of Life*. It was a collection of lectures from United Research. Jim Goure had given the lectures before he left the planet in the nineteen-eighties. The book was on the coffee table next to my meditation chair. I picked up the book, asked the Divine White Light to guide me to the right page, opened the book, and read:

CREATING GOOD

"We know everything there is to know about good and evil. We are able to judge what is right and what is wrong. But the Tree of Life is not involved in any way with a judgment of anyone or anything. That's why Jesus gave us that particular commandment, "Thou shalt not judge," because so much of our time is involved with judging and because that's what keeps us from climbing the Tree of Life.

The Bookstore- United Research
Black Mountain, N.C., 28711

For years, my cousin and my daughter have been telling me that I was very judgmental. I never really listened. Now I had to thank them, the entity, Jim Goure, and the Mother, for helping me realize the huge obstacle that was blocking my spiritual growth. I called up my loving cousin and thanked her for putting a mirror in front of me so I could look at my own reflection. If you want to learn a quick lesson, hurt someone in your own family. It is an immediate wake-up call. I don't recommend it, unless you want to know the meaning of the word "suffer."

That night before I went to bed, I talked to the entity. I thanked the entity for helping me to see that I was wrong in judging his house. I told him he didn't have to worry about his house anymore because the family that was going to move in loved his house. They would take care of it as carefully as his family had done. With this assurance, he could now concentrate on his new house. Also, he should be prepared for them to make some changes because everyone has different ideas about how to decorate. I wanted him not to get upset if they might find it necessary to redo some of his work. I thanked him for the perfect condition of the house. It was neat and clean, ready for immediate occupancy. I said I would send a bouquet of roses on my cousin's birthday so she could take them to the new house to celebrate this wonderful occasion. I said goodbye, have a wonderful life, and thank you.

I wrote a letter to my cousin but she never read it. I mailed it to her, but when it arrived, she was busy moving things into the new house. She may have known better than to open it when she was tired. The letter got lost. A few months later, when she had been at her house for three weeks, the two of us went out for lunch. She said, "I want to congratulate you for no longer being judgmental. I wish my husband and my daughters were here for this conversation because we have all noticed the difference in your new attitude." I emotionally patted myself on the back, smiled to her, and said, "Thank you, that recognition is very important to me for my spiritual development."

Synchronism

You may be wondering how you come to recognize when you are moving in the direction of a more spiritual life. The first thing that happens is you want to change your life style. You have the feeling that you are chasing yourself in circles and going nowhere. Something is missing and you can't figure out what it is, you can't put your finger on it. If you become sincere in wanting to change, you need to begin to carefully watch yourself. Day and night, watch how you react to everything.

I started to become aware of a change happening in my life while listening to the songs I caught myself singing. These had to be songs I hadn't heard while listening to the radio. They were songs I sang while painting watercolors or doing housework; I could read my moods by the words in the songs. It was a call for help from within. My inner self (witness or soul), was sending me personal messages and they surfaced in, of all things, a song. It begins to become interesting because, without realizing it, you find yourself humming old songs, new songs, all songs. You love it because you enjoy listening to yourself and you are often surprised at what you hear.

I am thoroughly convinced that your soul wants you to wake up. It is ready to help you upon the slightest invitation. It will meet you more than halfway. As I see it, we all have a color-coded guide that is patiently waiting to be of service to each of us. Your guide will be available to you if you sincerely ask for help, it has to, thats its purpose. However, you must understand that it knows the rules of your game. I see each lifetime as one big game. Each person follows his/her own rules. As an individual, I check out the games of other people. I decide whether I want to play with them because of their rules. Over time, I direct my own lifetime movie.

When I am sincere with my request for help, small things begin to happen. The right friend will come into my life. I might think of a certain person and they will phone or show up. I begin to notice that these things are more than coincidence. Soon, many things happen for right reasons and I dare to believe they are happening for me. In my case, after the things listed above, the numbers 17 and 7 popped into my awareness. The Mother guides me with these numbers. It took a long time and many different experiences before I realized that, although She was no longer in Her body, She still guides me. It may sound spooky, but by now I live knowing that She is always with me. She uses the number seven to get my attention when She wants me to carefully observe the situation in front of me. (Sri Aurobindo came to me on 7/07/67, my age-37.) If She uses the number seventeen, I become aware of a temporary happening in my life. Years after the death of my first child, I remembered that her birthday was September 17.

Let me give you a small for-instance. I was looking for a piece of property along a Michigan river. I had found exactly what I was looking for, but wasn't sure if I should buy it because it was four hours away from home and I wondered if I should buy it with a friend. It would be a weekend retreat. We saw it on a Sunday afternoon and decided to wait until we got home before we gave the realtor a definite decision. That evening, we called back and told him that we wanted to purchase the land. The realtor said we still had the first chance for buying it, but after we left, someone else had given him a check to hold it in case we didn't take it. If we wanted the land, we had one week to sign papers and get the first payment to his office. He had my address and would get the papers in the mail the following Monday morning. Each day I waited for the mail. Wednesday, Thursday, Friday came and no mail had arrived. Late Friday afternoon, we called and asked about the papers. They had been sent on Monday morning. He was waiting for us to reply. I asked what address he had mailed them to, and his answer showed that his secretary had made a mistake with the house number. Instead of a 2, she had written a 7. Our papers had gone to the Gas Company and they were closed until the following Monday. As soon as I heard the number seven, I laughed with joy because I knew the Mother was involved. She was saying, "Not this property." Within two weeks, we bought land near home.

Two years ago, my daughter called me. She wanted my advice as an ex-school teacher. Selena had an objection to a class assignment for my granddaughter in fifth grade. The assignment involved the legend of King Arthur. I gave her suggestions about how to approach the teacher and resolve the issue. Through that exchange, I learned things about King Arthur that I had never known and this leads into a story about synchronism.

During this same time, I was taking a course at a local church entitled, "Metaphor and the Bible." An Egyptian gentleman was in the class. After class, as we walked next to each other on the way to the parking lot, we talked about Coptic Christians. The Coptic Church Service is the same today as it was in the time of Jesus. He informed me that there were weekly Sunday Coptic Church services in a town twenty minutes away. I asked him for the address. He couldn't remember it, but he said he would leave a message on my memory call. He didn't call and wasn't in class the following week, so I couldn't get the information. I was leaving the area soon and wanted to see this church before I left, so I called a Coptic friend in Michigan to see if he could help me. He didn't have a list of Coptic Churches in America because he was the leader of a Mystical Coptic Organization and they were a separate group. He said, "It is strange that you should call because I recently asked a few of your friends for your address, but they didn't know where you were. We are having a group of healers travel to Merlin's cave in England to ground the feminine force. Because of your ties with the Mother, I thought you might want to join us." I thanked him and said I wasn't interested in visiting England because I had lived there for two years, and spending that much money I wanted to see some place I hadn't been to before. He sent me the tour leaflets anyway.

The tour would leave on July 17 and would stay five days in the King Arthur Hotel in Cornwall. When I saw the date 7/17, I thought, "Is it possible that the Mother wants me to go on this trip?" When the mail arrived the next day, a tri-monthly publication from a spiritual group in Tennessee had a review of three books by Lawrence Gardner: *King Arthur-Blood Line of the Holy Grail, Genesis of the Grail Kings, and Realm of the Ring Lords*. My car couldn't get me to the bookstore fast enough. This had to be more than coincidence. The three books were on the shelf. I browsed through each of them while having a cup of coffee at the bookshop café. As I left, I bought a copy of *King Arthur-Bloodline of the Holy Grail*. Little did I know that, over the next two days, when I got home, I would be glued to the lounge chair on my balcony while reading it, and even longer after purchasing the next two books.

Each passing day, the last day to register for the upcoming trip with the healers was closing in on me. One more direct indication from the Mother was what I needed to convince me She wanted me to join the group. While reading the third book, the "Go!" sign appeared. The flowers on the shield of King Arthur were the lily and the rose, the identical flowers besides "Intimate Relation," which I had handed the Mother. I figured that was the positive signal I had been waiting for. Now I was convinced that I had better not lose this chance to serve Her. The bank made out a loan and I phoned in my down payment for a fifteen day trip to Tintagal in Cornwall, England.

For the ceremony at Merlin's cave, I needed a white dress, a white lily, and a peach rose. The King Arthur Castle/Hotel was located near a small, isolated village so I wasn't sure that I would be near a place to buy flowers. I searched in West Palm Beach for card shops where one could find lovely, hand painted pictures that could be cut and placed on my 8'x12' plastic coated portrait of the Mother (plastic coated because it would be placed on the sand near the sea). The paintings would have been more personal if I had painted them, but I hadn't had a brush in my hands since 1985.

By the time the trip to England materialized, I wasn't sure that I could make it. I had made my last payment before I found out that I had cancer and it was too late for a refund (even if you have cancer!). For months, the doctors had examined me and were without a diagnosis as to what type of cancer it was. My next appointment with them was in three weeks, so they gave me permission to go on the trip (if I didn't exert myself). I flew to England and joined the group. When the healers heard my scenario, they unanimously responded with, 'No way". These wonderful women daily took turns surrounding me with their loving vibrations. I'll never know if that female spiritual experience resulted for me in Level 1- Non Aggressive Cancer.

New Age Sex

For many people, one of the major stumbling blocks for following the path of Integral Yoga seems to be the matter of dealing with the sexual urges of human beings. Sri Aurobindo and the Mother believed preservation of sex-energy was needed for the transformation of human consciousness and Their Ashram was founded on the aim of spiritual transformation. Auroville is also founded on the Integral Yoga of Sri Aurobindo and the Mother, and the aim also is spiritual transformation. But many Aurovillians establish their own rules regarding sexual behavior. In the past, some Ashramites questioned the Mother about the validity of this double standard of rules. They wondered why She allowed people like "hippies," who disregarded all rules, to live there. The Mother explained that everyone on the planet needed to make the transition (*The Hundredth Monkey*), and individuals will recognize the need to conserve this energy as they progress to a higher consciousness while moving along the path. Sexual activity seems to be one of the biggest games on the transformation score board. Each person keeps his/her own secret score card which, in turn, makes them alone responsible for their own growth and development.

My introduction to the fact that people were looking for alternatives to a normal sexual relationship happened at least twenty years ago at that SFF Conference, when I first met Jim Goure. He announced, on the first day of our scheduled meetings, that Thursday would be the best-attended workshop of the conference because the topic would be New Age Sex. Along with him, we all had a good laugh. He was going to show us how to have a "quickie" with a stranger and not make our mate jealous. We had another good laugh.

He was right-on. Thursday morning, the small, college, lecture hall was full of joyous people with high hopes of learning something altogether new. I was seated high up in an aisle seat, almost in the last row. The place was packed with all ages of SFF members. He began the lecture by explaining that, in the future, humanity would no longer have physical sexual contact. There might not even be reproductive organs on the body.

In his typical, humorous, Jim Goure style, he announced, "We're not at that stage yet so, never fear, New Age Sex is still better than ever!" Demonstrating with a thrust of his hands, palms up, he held up both hands, and said, "With these, you don't even need to undress, and it will only take a few minutes of your lunch break. It's better than lunch!"

While he continued to talk to the crowd, as if propelled by a puppeteer, I stood up and started walking down the stairs and up the aisle to the stage. To this day, I don't know what possessed me, because I am usually quite shy in the company of strangers. I now believe it was the Mother wanting me to have this experience. As I was walking, I heard Jim say, "I'll need a volunteer. Oh, here she comes right now!" I walked up to the stage and stood next to Jim. He asked my name and said something like, "You can even have sex with a stranger."

Jim showed the audience how to place his hands, while facing me, on the top of mine. He told me to close my eyes and concentrate on sending positive energy. After what seemed like a few minutes, but enough time to focus, we opened our eyes and dropped our hands to our sides. He said, "That's it folks, that's all it takes." He thanked me for being his partner. As I returned to my seat, he added, "If she were my wife, we would continue this act in bed. You remove your clothes and, for a while, front-to-front you hold palms together, then turn on your side and place your spines back to back. You must get as close as possible and concentrate on slowly sending vibrations up and down your spine!" There was a question and answer period, and we were dismissed for lunch. The people sitting next to me wanted to know what I felt. I honestly answered, "Nothing," and left the building.

There was a long line at the lunch counter. Acquaintances from the conference were busy discussing the lecture, but my sensitized mind began to float. Passing the cafeteria line without stopping, because the food looked too heavy to digest, I re-stacked my tray and went to my room in the dorm. Resting on the twin bed didn't work either, so I went outside and stood in front of the dormitory in the noon sun.

Across the street was a clump of shade trees that lined a tucked away tree arbor with a circular sidewalk. Crossing over, I seated myself on a cement bench. That action lasted two seconds, so taking off my shoes, and getting back on my feet, I started to stroll around and around on the flower-lined path. My steps were as light as a feather. I felt like a fairy princess slowly twirling while dancing on tip-toes. Each bounce brought forth a magical leap and with a musical, "la, la, lee," words tumbled from my endless song. I drifted completely outside of myself. This body lilted around with laughter in my heart and with a constant grin on my face. I had no weight or thoughts and no boundary to the velvet air that surrounded me. I watched and waited as words of a poem written years before slowly sprang from my whispering lips. "Flowers of air fall on my face and I have been kissed by the Gods." Dispersing a few, "la, la, lees," between the words of the poem, and in a state of rapture, I danced and sang, nonstop for the next hour (perhaps more). Inside of me, the Gods, the Mother, and Jim surely fused in delightful delirium.

Soon the auditorium doors on the other side of the lawn opened and people from the conference were leaving the lecture hall. I couldn't let them observe me acting like a slowly whirling dervisher, so coming to my senses, I realized I had to come down to reality. What a mistake that was! Perhaps I could have stayed there forever! I figured the only way to get grounded was to touch the earth, so I placed myself on my back upon the soft green grass. With arms and legs outstretched like a snow angel, I rested for another hour. In the atmosphere of peaceful silence, with birds chirping and lofty clouds above, I lay with eyes opening and closing as circles of rainbow colors left my body to disappear forever. All the while, my murmuring mind repeated again and again, "Oh Joy! Thank you, Jim!"

Stairway to Paradise

Perhaps some of you remember a movie when the Frenchman Maurice Chevalier sang a song called "Stairway to Paradise." The words went something like this, "We'll build a stairway to paradise with a new step every day." He sang and danced on each step as he slowly ascended and descended the stairs. The words of this song, in a nutshell, for me, are the history of our evolutionary patterns. We are all, like it or not, in spite of ourselves, climbing stairs to paradise and most of us are not aware of the climb. Sometimes we step up and at other times we step down, perhaps more than we want to, but in the long run we are slowly progressing toward moving ourselves forward, I think, toward enlightenment. To me, that is why the voice told me that, "Everyone is going to become a Jesus."

In this book, I am trying to convey to each of you that I have found that it is possible to climb faster, much faster. Everything seen above, below, in front of, and behind you is on a step. A step that is a color-coded, energized movement; even when you fall down, it is a movement (a lesson) toward a higher consciousness. The way to reach the goal of a step upward is through the practice of Integral Yoga. This method of yoga leads one to meditation, which is the process to silence the mind, and a silenced mind makes it possible for you to become aware of the Spirit (soul) within.

To further explain some of the steps one has to take, I'll try to relate my conception of the steps as energy. This energy is an ocean of Oneness. Perhaps it's Light, Spirit, Truth-consciousness, or something else. With an explosion like the Big Bang, you may have shot off from your mother of Oneness and then begun your individual search to eventually return to her, your original source. You began from something as small as, or smaller than, an atom or particle of dust. You were energy that formed into a force field or collective (through time) mass. This mass was always in a state of attracting, detracting, or rest, but always in a state of developing. Energy is color-coded, so as you developed, you changed colors and your vibration changed. That centralized, vibratory, whirl of concentrated energy, that one day would become you, began to attract and mingle with higher intensities of consciousness. You went through the stage of everything that is found in this Universe. You were that grain of sand, mud, weeds, plants, animals, until you became a human.

Up to that time, you existed on the level of your particular color-coded, vibratory intensity. For instance, when you were an animal, you were guided by a group soul. You relied on instinct. Cats, dogs, birds, whatever animal, instinctively know how to grow and develop because of the level of their vibrations, which, in turn, is a level of consciousness. They have a mind, but they are not aware that they have one. Humans realize they have a mind. They can think and, because they have the capacity to think, they have the capacity to develop the mind.

The record of how the mind developed is located within a vibratory group soul. That record stays with us from lifetime to lifetime. First, we developed a mind for our physical body. As we further developed, we made a mind for our emotional body, and, last but not least, a mind for our mental body. These minds are patterns of past habits that control our every action until we learn to quiet them. When a mind is balanced and quiet, we find that we are really not these minds. We are energy that is trying to separate from this throbbing, engulfing, saturating whirl of possessiveness that controls each of us. In order to do so, we must become aware that within, hidden (because of the clatter), is to be found our individual Divine Soul.

Sri Aurobindo now enters our picture. Every night on a news program of Indian Television, before the program begins, they present flashes of faces that are important to the history of India. Sri Aurobindo is one of those faces. In the past, after leaving England, He was a revolutionary working for the freedom of India. During that time, He was imprisoned for one year. While in prison, He read the religious books of India, and had a visitation from Vivekananda, a deceased holy man of the Ramakrishna order of Monks. Vivekananda stayed with Him for two weeks while He imparted His knowledge to Him. In His cell, Sri Aurobindo experienced all the lower levels of consciousness.

I don't know if you have ever looked back on the history of the human race, or the evolution of the survival of the fittest, but I frequently have to remind myself of how fortunate I am to be alive today. I realize that in other lifetimes I may have witnessed horrid human behavior. I shudder each time I think of the French guillotine, throwing humans into the lion's den, and burning people at the stake. Sri Aurobindo, in His cell, descended and suffered greatly as He experienced all that has ever happened throughout the evolutionary past. At the pit of the experience, He came to a breakthrough of White Light. There is light above, below, and to the sides of darkness. We are, in reality, boxed in by light and White Light is Divine Spirit or Truth-Consciousness.

When Sri Aurobindo left prison, He moved to the French occupied section of India, to the city of Pondicherry. He and a few of His devotees lived together in a small house and were safe from searches of the British Police. Sometime later, the Mother and Her husband came to visit Him. She immediately recognized Sri Aurobindo as a figure who repeatedly had come to Her as a vision in Paris. Four years later, She decided to stay in Pondicherry to work with Him and His handful of devotees. Eventually, She organized the Ashram. While the Mother took charge of the various activities of the Ashram, Sri Aurobindo lived for twenty-four years in isolation in one of the apartments in the main house. His goal was to experience and, hence, establish here on earth a higher level of consciousness which He accomplished!

Before He went to prison, Sri Aurobindo learned to silence His mind. This goal sometimes took others a lifetime to attain, but He, with the help of a guru, did it in three days. He was able to see and divert thoughts from entering into His head. During His time in prison, He had descended into the mire of the mind. Now, in Southern India, in isolation, He ascended the steps beyond the mind.

Knowing the function of the mind (minds) is the key to understanding who you are. It is possible to become aware of the fact that each of us can advance to a greater, higher knowledge of the working of the mind. Our ordinary mind is an evolution of the past. It is full of thoughts. It is a cloudy mind that only thinks in unconnected spurts or limitations.

In the ongoing evolution, according to Sri Aurobindo, we will evolve onto higher levels of mind because of different intensities of energy, levels of color, and degrees of consciousness. Each of the higher minds responds to Light.

Our Ordinary Mind is a part of the evolution of the earth and at the top of the head, above this earth-mind, is found a great divide (Vijnana). To get to the spiritual side of the divide, consciousness must cross over a bridge to enter into the realm of higher minds. There are four minds that rise, one above the other, because of greater degrees of Light. Sri Aurobindo calls these: Higher Mind, Illumined Mind, Intuitive Mind, and Overmind, or Cosmic Consciousness. *Each mind is dancing to the energy of one step beyond the other.*

Golden Jubilee

For this chapter, I would like to take you into my mind because I am trying to explain something that for years, to me, has been practically incomprehensible. To begin to understand Sri Aurobindo and the Mother, one needs to go to a place beyond the mind. When Sri Aurobindo took me to that patch of blue and said, "That is the only ability available to your mind," I thought who dares to go beyond the mind, and if I did dare, where would it take me? How do I get there and how do I get back? My first reaction was, "I would go crazy if I lost my mind!" Years later, while thinking about the same statement, I thought, "He must mean one needs to go through or use the mind to get beyond the mind, but where is the passage? How does one begin to go beyond or through your own mind?"

To begin this quest, I invite you to enter into my thoughts of the time when I was about eight or nine years old. I was sitting on the steps of the front porch, watering the lawn with a long, black hose. Watering the lawn was one of the ways I earned my weekly allowance. I was bored and as I looked at the grass and trees, I said to myself, "Who named grass, grass and tree, tree? Why isn't tree, grass and grass, tree?" This is important for my story only because it is the first time I remember being inquisitive about the unknown.

At age eleven, I remember sitting at a cottage along a small lake that opened into Lake Michigan. As I sat in a big, painted, wooden lawn chair, watching the night sky, I wondered if what I had been told about the stars could possibly be true. "Are there really as many stars in the sky as there are grains of sand on all the beaches on the planet earth?" It seemed incredible that there might be as many stars as there are grains of sand. Lake Michigan was full of beaches and sand dunes. I had been to Florida and seen many more beaches. I can remember running those small grains through my fingers and trying to imagine how many millions, billions, trillions might be found on just one beach. Were adults crazy with their tales about the stars in the sky? But why would they lie?

This leads me into the main reason I am telling you this story. I don't know how old I was when I was told, or as I read in a book, that when a tiny or microscopic germ or bug looked up into my body, it would see what I see as I looked up at stars and planets in the night sky. It would see space and whirling planets or galaxies. This thought led me to imagine that what I was looking up at in the dark sky was the body of a huge female being who was pregnant with the planet earth, and that when earth becomes a perfected planet, when we all loved our neighbor as ourselves, we would be birthed into a larger space or another universe (maybe through a black hole)!

Why did I bring this to your attention? Because I think it will help me better explain how I see what Sri Aurobindo is saying about our mind. Let's say that the people on the planet earth represent where the mind is in its development at this time. You now know that we have many minds that are whirling around inside of this one human body. Our job is to slowly unfurl these minds and see their actions as comprehensible units of colored energy. In order to go beyond this mind, we have to complete our evolutionary journey. We must perfect or balance the different levels, colors, vibrations, energies (call them what you will), so that one day humans will be birthed by this female consciousness (Shakti), to cross over the color-coded bridge to Oneness. Sri Aurobindo calls that achievement; arriving at the (Supermind), Supramental Consciousness or Truth-Consciousness.

We humans need to recognize that we in our evolutionary plan to be re-birthed into Spirit or Oneness are only at the halfway point, some more advanced than others. According to the Mother, in the overall plan, we can compare ourselves, at this stage of our development, to the time when the fish climbed out of the sea, which means we have a very long way to go. You ask for a path. There is no path, because each of us have our individual vibrating mass of energies to deal (incubate) with so we make our own path.

Our minds have, throughout evolution, formed the habit of control and we need to reverse that process and take back our lives, or better stated, take back our minds. We are mind-controlled puppets with bad habits and are led around like blind sheep. It is time for us to wake up! So for the good of humanity, Sri Aurobindo and the Mother devoted Their lives to showing us the way. They offered to us an example of what life could be like. They experimented and didn't teach anything that They personally had not achieved. Sri Aurobindo lived in seclusion while He worked on crossing the bridge and bringing to earth the Golden Light of the Supramental potential for all human beings.

During those twenty-four years of seclusion, He described in His writing, the step-by-step levels of the advanced stages of the evolution of the mind that we humans will one day evolve through and to (I have mentioned these earlier). At the height of this experience, we will enter into a Golden Light. His and the Mother's work brought down the vibration of that light to the planet earth. They devoted Their lives to showing and telling us what it is and how to attain it. He wrote that if 12 sadhaks (practitioners of Integral Yoga) could attain this degree of advancement, the vibration would be grounded on earth. Unfortunately, that hasn't happened yet. This resonated, as I read it, to the story of the Hundredth Monkey and the Morphogenetic Fields Theory.

Sri Aurobindo left His body on December 5, 1950. For five days His body lay in His room, on His bed, from the morning of December 5th, until He was interred on the 9th. In the heat of India, a body is usually buried within hours, but this body glowed with such light that it didn't begin to decompose. The French Government became concerned and sent a representative to examine the situation. They were amazed and agreed to wait for the Light to slowly fade away. A friend of mine, who has lived at the Ashram since he was a small child, witnessed that Light. "Even as an eight year old, I could not miss the brightly lit body of His. I recall touching the feet. They were soft as butter." Only on the 8th one could see the normal skin color and the normal disfigurement that follows the death of a body."

Sri Aurobindo, before, had merged His Light with the Mother's Light. He related to Her that Her physical body was stronger than His. He said He would pass over to do the work on the other side. It would be up to Her to experience the grounding of this Supramental Light. That happened on February 29, 1956, at the Ashram playground, the day of the Celebration of the GOLDEN JUBILEE.

The Awakening

An American guru, whom I greatly respected, once told me he thought the reason that I had traveled around most of the globe and had lived in so many places was because I was revisiting former lifetimes. Somehow, intuitively, it made sense to me because I have had that same feeling about reviewing places in this life. In America, I have lived in Michigan, Chicago, Virginia Beach, Miami, New York, New Jersey, San Francisco, Oceanside, CA, and now South Palm Beach. I have retraced many of my former steps and as I returned to most of these places, I usually searched, and almost always found, the location of where many of these memories had taken place. Sometimes I sat in front of a house or in a coffee shop remembering all the good and bad times. I left the scene saying, "Good-bye! That's the end of that! Thanks for the experience!" I could feel myself completing or releasing a uniting circle of past vibrations. I went home, showered, scrubbed away all dead skin cells, washed my hair, and ended up freely dancing around the hotel room singing, "YES! YES! Oh, YES!"

Sri Aurobindo, when He came to me, said, "The Agony of your life is over." Somehow, and I don't know why, that intuitively also makes sense. I guess I have to live longer to find out what that may mean. My life has been very different from anyone I have ever known. I often doubted if I even belonged on this planet. As I think back on my childhood, I wonder if I felt that way back then. I can remember sitting on the edge of my bed, wishing I could find a zipper that extended from my toes to my head. I wanted to unzip my skin so the real "me" could step out. I also remember in 1967 (once again, 1967), the time when I had a corneal transplant (new vision) on my left eye. The doctor said to me as he held my hands, "You are like a bird in a cage, just waiting for someone to open the door and let you fly out."

Frequently my feeling was like being a balloon floating just above the skyline of the city. I always felt secure because someone held the string that brought me back to earth. Whenever I was needed at home, I was called or pulled back. Once my divorce was over, it took a long time to resettle because there was no one to hold the string, so grounding and floating was no longer a way of living.

Writing this book has grounded me in a new way. Layer by layer, I have been forced to revaluate, understand, and dissolve some of the powers of unknown vibrations that have driven me from one episode to another. One of the biggest mysteries as I look back on it is the fact that I came from such a religious background, but never felt spiritual. It wasn't until I read the work of Sri Aurobindo and the Mother, with a reference to God as having other names, like White Light, Oneness, Divine, Truth-Consciousness, Spirit and the Supramental, that I found an avenue to follow, in order to find a new meaning in my blindly driven life.

I vividly remember the first time I was told about the full meaning of the term "reincarnation". I was clearly amazed that I hadn't heard about it before. I thought to myself, "How much time have I wasted by not knowing this? Why on earth did my religion hide this information from me, and all the other members of my church? What was it they were trying to hide?" With that new picture of my surroundings and the world around me, I viewed life as a continuous progression of events. At long last, the extreme strangeness of my unusual life began to fit together and make some kind of sense.

I became aware of the fact that I knew little about the whole picture of the huge puzzle of life and lifetimes. With a renewed sense of energy and an invigorated inquisitiveness or rebirth, my search began. I could comfortably, but ever so slowly, zip off the outer layer of old skin and hope for the caged bird to take flight.

I had touched a White Light of Oneness while soaring over the waves and surging up, up, and up until merging with, "A Peace that Passes Understanding." It hadn't occurred to me that this might be a religious experience. I just bathed in the vibration of other worldliness. Now that I have read about Nirvana, I wonder if that is what I touched. Either way, in the long run (a very long run), it was a consequence of insignificance because the purpose of feeling Oneness is to be able to go there as frequently as you like and to stay as long as you choose. I could do neither.

I had been fortunate enough to have experienced that glorious feeling of Light and, because of it, knew what to aspire for during the remaining years of this life. The question remained: How do I get there? What is the path? I found, after many false trials and tribulations, the best way for me is through the Integral Yoga of Sri Aurobindo. His yoga is different from all other yoga because other yoga teaches you to leave your body to attain Nirvana. Sri Aurobindo says, "Transform the body!" Other yoga teaches us that their methods are also through yoga, but the difference is that they begin to uncurl the energy from the lower chakras (colors of energy), and Sri Aurobindo says we begin at the top of the head and lower ourselves slowly, so as not to get caught and spend energy (sometimes lifetimes) at one basic lower level.

Sri Aurobindo also said reaching Nirvana is not enough. There are higher levels of consciousness. You don't leave your body, you change it, you spiritualize it! You begin with meditation because eventually that leads to perfect silence. As you develop a still mind, the outcome will make room for the White Light to slowly transform your vibrations, colors, and consciousness. Once you decide to make an earnest attempt to develop to a higher level, Spirit will automatically extend a helping hand, a spark that equalizes your effort as you help yourself. Your goal is to light the flame to become aware of your individual soul or, as Sri Aurobindo calls it, your Psychic Being.

When you ignite the flame (red spark) of your soul, you begin the inner work. Your goal is to cross the rainbow bridge. The bridge leads from leaving the animal–human nature to becoming a spiritualized being. Your eventual reward is Oneness or at-one-ment (atonement). Every day of your life, you take one step toward the crossing. Sometimes you step forward and at other times, step back. The journey is long and the obstacles to confront are extreme. Your desire to develop into a spiritualized Light must become steadfast: To grow, to become aware, to understand the functions of mental, emotional, and physical mind, ego, pride, lust (just for starters).

Once again, we return to the topic of being creative. We must dare to step into the unknown. We need to blaze a new trail, a trail that will individually lead us to merge with Oneness. Since Sri Aurobindo came to me, I feel that His method of the practice of Integral Yoga is the path for me. It may not be the one for you. Jesus and other enlightened beings had a path. Those paths over the past generations came to show us what joy, peace, and love is awaiting mankind.

Truth-Consciousness is a precious gift you are able to give to yourself. It is a gift of loving yourself. You are not alone. Within you is an energized seed (Light) that understands the history of your entire evolutionary journey. It seems to be like the DNA that traces us back to Eve. If you desire White Light, you must equal that expectation with the faith that it can and will happen. Every moment is an opportunity for you to express that faith. In time, perhaps much time, it will be a new code or a new form of your daily existence. In India, it is labeled Satchitananda. I have just realized that we already have Sat-existence, Chit-consciousness, and what we are longing for is Ananda-Joy, Peace, Bliss, and Delight!

To find Peace, we need to challenge ourselves to enjoy each day of our life. No one wants to be around us if we are unhappy and bitter. Like attracts like, or as I said before, Light attracts Light. Let your personal Self shine because you are Light, A

Bright Shiny Light! Find the good, positiveness, and love in life, and that feeling of joy will surely reflect back on you. With the ending of this book, I would hope that we leave with the thought that there is more to life than living as we now live. Be open to it and allow yourself to reveal its wonder!

..................OM SHANTI..................

"A new world, based on truth and refusing the old slavery to falsehood, wants to take birth. In all countries there are people who know it, at least feel it. To them we call: Will you collaborate?"

Words of the Mother CWM 15, p.167

Summary

So what have I learned during the process of finding myself? As a right-brained person, I need to see the big, as it turns out, very big overall picture of what life is about. I will keep this in simple terms because that is what I believe is necessary. For me, civilization has made this entire story an exaggerated, exhausting, fragmentation of a simple plan. It seems to me that Einstein, by showing a relationship between energy and matter, has said it all. Everything that we see and feel is energy. My history is (as is yours), one of descending involution and ascending evolution.

I am energy that has somehow become separated from White Light. Once separated, my task is to find my way back to where I started. This is a spiritual undertaking. I became gross matter and now have started a journey of becoming Light. In the process, I developed an ego which, without realizing it, made me believe that I was separate from all that is surrounding me. Now I need to dissolve that ego in order to fuse back into the Light. My ego is tied up in my mind. The development of the three different minds (physical, emotional, and mental), as separate energies which show the history of how I got to where I am now. The question remains, how do I return?

The Integral Yoga of Sri Aurobindo and the Mother (They are One Light), shows me the direction of the path. One must silence the mind (meditation) because a cluttered mind doesn't allow White Light to fully penetrate into it. The more you silence your mind, the more light can enter and guide your life. Just like we are what we eat, we are what we think. If you want to know who you are, *stop all that thinking!* Sri Aurobindo stopped thoughts from entering His mind in three days! Thoughts are what clutter the mind.

With the writing of this book, I now realize that I have put my ego on the line. I have, hopefully, exposed it and thereby am beginning to become aware of my own game. I have done it my way by taking Sri Aurobindo seriously when He expressed that one should step into the mire and seed Light. When I met the Mother, I offered this instrument (me) to help do Her work on this physical plane. One can become a devout follower, but to bathe in the mire, as you have read in this book, is not an easy task. My hope is to:

Open the cage door of past thoughts
Let the blue bird soar
Find the way back to become One with the Light
Return to my Spiritual home.

Suggested Reading

* *Sri Aurobindo-or THE ADVENTURE OF CONSCIOUSNESS-*
Satprem
ISBN 81-85137-60-9

*THE MIND OF CELLS-
Satprem I
SBN 2-902776-60-8 & 81-85137-50-1

*THE MOTHER-The Story of Her Life-
Georges Van Vrekhem
ISBN-81-7223-416-3

> **PURCHASE AT:*
> **Auromere, 2621 West Highway 12,*
> *Lodi, CA 95242, U.S.A.*
> **Matagiri Sri Aurobindo Center*
> *1218 Wittenberg Road*
> *Mount Tremper, NY 12457*

A NEW SCIENCE OF LIFE –
The Hypothesis of Formative Causation
ISBN 0-87477-459-4 (pbk.)
Rupert Sheldrake- Jeremy P. Tarcher, INC. Los Angles

THE RAINBOW BRIDGE-
First and Second Phases- Link with the Soul--Purification
By Two Disciples-The Triune Foundation-P.O. Box226
Escondido, CA 92025
ISBN 0-87613-078-3